OPPOSING
VIEWPOINTS®
SERIES

Government Gridlock

Other Books of Related Interest:

Opposing Viewpoints Series

The Democratic Party

The Republican Party

At Issue Series

The Affordable Care Act

Health Care Legislation

What Is the Future of the US Economy?

Current Controversies Series

Politics and Media

Politics and Religion

Social Security

"Congress shall make no law . . . abridging the freedom of speech, or of the press."

First Amendment to the US Constitution

The basic foundation of our democracy is the First Amendment guarantee of freedom of expression. The Opposing Viewpoints series is dedicated to the concept of this basic freedom and the idea that it is more important to practice it than to enshrine it.

Government Gridlock

Margaret Haerens, Book Editor

GREENHAVEN PRESS
A part of Gale, Cengage Learning

Farmington Hills, Mich • San Francisco • New York • Waterville, Maine
Meriden, Conn • Mason, Ohio • Chicago

Patricia Coryell, *Vice President & Publisher, New Products & GVRL*
Douglas Dentino, *Manager, New Products*
Judy Galens, *Acquisitions Editor*

LIBRARY OF CONGRESS CATALOGING-IN-PUBLICATION DATA

Government gridlock / edited by Margaret Haerens.
    pages cm. -- (Opposing viewpoints)
    Summary: "Opposing Viewpoints: Government Gridlock: Opposing Viewpoints is the leading source for libraries and classrooms in need of current-issue materials. The viewpoints are selected from a wide range of highly respected sources and publications"-- Provided by publisher.
    Includes bibliographical references and index.
    ISBN 978-0-7377-7266-1 (hardback) -- ISBN 978-0-7377-7267-8 (paperback)
    1. Filibusters (Political science)--United States--Juvenile literature. 2. Divided government--United States--United States--Juvenile literature. I. Haerens, Margaret.
    JF519.G68 2015
    320.473'04--dc23
                                                    2014035339

Printed in the United States of America
1 2 3 4 5 6 7 19 18 17 16 15

Contents

Chapter 3: How Should Government Gridlock Be Addressed?

Chapter 4: How Will Filibuster Reform Impact Government Gridlock?

Why Consider Opposing Viewpoints?

> *"The only way in which a human being can make some approach to knowing the whole of a subject is by hearing what can be said about it by persons of every variety of opinion and studying all modes in which it can be looked at by every character of mind. No wise man ever acquired his wisdom in any mode but this."*
>
> John Stuart Mill

In our media-intensive culture it is not difficult to find differing opinions. Thousands of newspapers and magazines and dozens of radio and television talk shows resound with differing points of view. The difficulty lies in deciding which opinion to agree with and which "experts" seem the most credible. The more inundated we become with differing opinions and claims, the more essential it is to hone critical reading and thinking skills to evaluate these ideas. Opposing Viewpoints books address this problem directly by presenting stimulating debates that can be used to enhance and teach these skills. The varied opinions contained in each book examine many different aspects of a single issue. While examining these conveniently edited opposing views, readers can develop critical thinking skills such as the ability to compare and contrast authors' credibility, facts, argumentation styles, use of persuasive techniques, and other stylistic tools. In short, the Opposing Viewpoints Series is an ideal way to attain the higher-level thinking and reading skills so essential in a culture of diverse and contradictory opinions.

In addition to providing a tool for critical thinking, Opposing Viewpoints books challenge readers to question their own strongly held opinions and assumptions. Most people form their opinions on the basis of upbringing, peer pressure, and personal, cultural, or professional bias. By reading carefully balanced opposing views, readers must directly confront new ideas as well as the opinions of those with whom they disagree. This is not to argue simplistically that everyone who reads opposing views will—or should—change his or her opinion. Instead, the series enhances readers' understanding of their own views by encouraging confrontation with opposing ideas. Careful examination of others' views can lead to the readers' understanding of the logical inconsistencies in their own opinions, perspective on why they hold an opinion, and the consideration of the possibility that their opinion requires further evaluation.

Evaluating Other Opinions

To ensure that this type of examination occurs, Opposing Viewpoints books present all types of opinions. Prominent spokespeople on different sides of each issue as well as well-known professionals from many disciplines challenge the reader. An additional goal of the series is to provide a forum for other, less known, or even unpopular viewpoints. The opinion of an ordinary person who has had to make the decision to cut off life support from a terminally ill relative, for example, may be just as valuable and provide just as much insight as a medical ethicist's professional opinion. The editors have two additional purposes in including these less known views. One, the editors encourage readers to respect others' opinions—even when not enhanced by professional credibility. It is only by reading or listening to and objectively evaluating others' ideas that one can determine whether they are worthy of consideration. Two, the inclusion of such viewpoints encourages the important critical thinking skill of objectively evaluating an author's credentials and bias. This evaluation will illuminate an author's reasons for taking a particular stance on an issue and will aid in readers' evaluation of the author's ideas.

It is our hope that these books will give readers a deeper understanding of the issues debated and an appreciation of the complexity of even seemingly simple issues when good and honest people disagree. This awareness is particularly important in a democratic society such as ours in which people enter into public debate to determine the common good. Those with whom one disagrees should not be regarded as enemies but rather as people whose views deserve careful examination and may shed light on one's own.

Thomas Jefferson once said that "difference of opinion leads to inquiry, and inquiry to truth." Jefferson, a broadly educated man, argued that "if a nation expects to be ignorant and free . . . it expects what never was and never will be." As individuals and as a nation, it is imperative that we consider the opinions of others and examine them with skill and discernment. The Opposing Viewpoints series is intended to help readers achieve this goal.

David L. Bender and Bruno Leone,
Founders

Introduction

> *"To what expedient, then, shall we finally resort, for maintaining in practice the necessary partition of power among the several departments, as laid down in the Constitution? The only answer that can be given is, that as all these exterior provisions are found to be inadequate, the defect must be supplied, by so contriving the interior structure of the government as that its several constituent parts may, by their mutual relations, be the means of keeping each other in their proper places."*
>
> —James Madison,
> "Federalist No. 51," 1788

On August 21, 2013, a group of eighty Republican congressmen sent a letter to Speaker of the House John Boehner urging him to take a political stand against funding of the Patient Protection and Affordable Care Act (PPACA), also known as the Affordable Care Act (ACA) or Obamacare, the 2010 health care law that was passed to expand access to health insurance and reduce the cost of health care for individuals and the government. Fiercely opposed to the PPACA, Republicans argued that Obamacare would actually increase costs, offer less choice for families and individuals, balloon the size and scope of the government, and present an unwelcome government intrusion into the lives of all Americans.

The letter proposed that until Republicans had the political power to fully repeal Obamacare—a move impossible while President Barack Obama was in office—they should work to defund the law.

A month later, Boehner and House Republicans put that plan into action, forcing a showdown on the debt ceiling in an attempt to bring down government spending and defund Obamacare.

In order to pay the nation's bills, Congress would have to raise the debt ceiling, which is the total amount of money that the US government can borrow. Raising the debt ceiling has become controversial in recent years; some fiscal conservatives view the process as evidence that the government is spending too much and reinforces the need to substantially cut spending.

There are many economists, however, who contend that raising the debt ceiling should not be used as a political tool because the money is financing existing obligations, such as Social Security and Medicare payments, military salaries, tax refunds, and ongoing scientific and medical research. Not raising the debt ceiling would mean defaulting on the nation's financial obligations, possibly causing catastrophic consequences on the US economy.

On September 21, 2013, the House passed an appropriations bill that would defund Obamacare but still provide funding to keep the government open until January. As expected, President Obama announced that he would veto any such bill if it came to his desk.

As a government shutdown loomed on October 1, Republicans doubled down on their attempts to defund Obamacare. On September 29, the House passed another spending bill. This version proposed to delay funding Obamacare for one year and repeal a medical device tax. A day later, the Senate stripped both conditions from the bill.

The day before the shutdown, the House passed a spending bill that would raise the debt ceiling but delay the health care mandate, a requirement in the PPACA that stipulated that most Americans obtain health insurance coverage by 2014 or pay a tax penalty. This version of the bill also required members of Congress and their staffs to give up their government-provided health insurance coverage and purchase new insurance from the PPACA exchanges, which offer a range of affordable health insurance options for small businesses, families, and individuals.

The Senate rejected this final House plan, setting the stage for a government shutdown the next day. As Congress scrambled to pass piecemeal legislation to continue paying US service members and civilian contractors, the political fallout from the debt-ceiling showdown intensified.

On the eve of the shutdown, President Obama urged Republicans to keep the government open and stop manufacturing crises to incite their political base. On October 1, 2013, the US government shut down: federal agencies and national parks closed; federally funded research stopped; economic assistance programs ran out of money; and many other important services were halted until a bill raising the debt ceiling was passed. Approximately eight hundred thousand federal workers were furloughed. Several thousand federal workers were deemed "essential" and were required to report to work, but they were not paid until the end of the shutdown.

Several days into the shutdown, House Speaker Boehner urged the president and Democratic leadership to negotiate with Republicans and insisted the central obstacle to a new appropriations bill was government spending. He argued that Republicans were not going to raise the debt ceiling without an agreement on substantial spending cuts. With pressure mounting over a fiscal default, House Republicans agreed to raise the debt ceiling on October 16. Federal employees went back to work the next day.

In later remarks, President Obama reflected on the cost of the government shutdown to US credibility and the nation's national and economic security. "Some of the same folks who pushed for the shutdown and threatened default claim their actions were needed to get America back on the right track, to make sure we're strong," he observed in his remarks. "But probably nothing has done more damage to America's credibility in the world, our standing with other countries, than the spectacle that we've seen these past several weeks. It's encouraged our enemies, it's emboldened our competitors, and it's depressed our friends, who look to us for steady leadership."

Months later, the financial ratings agency Standard & Poor's estimated that the shutdown cost the American economy approximately $24 billion. In another analysis of the effects of the shutdown, the Council of Economic Advisers estimated that the crisis resulted in 120,000 fewer private sector jobs.

The authors of the viewpoints in *Opposing Viewpoints: Government Gridlock* explore the causes and consequences of political gridlock in chapters titled "Is Government Gridlock a Serious Problem?," "What Are the Causes of Government Gridlock?," "How Should Government Gridlock Be Addressed?," and "How Will Filibuster Reform Impact Government Gridlock?" The information contained in this volume provides insight into the debate over the scope of government dysfunction, illuminates the role of the Tea Party and the media in facilitating political impasses, and presents different proposals to alleviate gridlock in the US government.

Is Government Gridlock a Serious Problem?

Chapter Preface

One recent consequence of the paralyzing gridlock witnessed in the US Congress is the sequester, or automatic budget cuts, that were implemented on March 1, 2013. These cuts will total around $1.2 trillion over the next decade, split evenly between domestic spending, such as Medicare and other programs, and defense spending. Social Security, Medicaid, Temporary Assistance for Needy Families (TANF, or welfare), and Supplemental Nutrition Assistance Program (SNAP, or food stamps) are exempt from automatic cuts.

The sequestration cuts generated bitter controversy. Supporters argued that they would help slash both the deficit and the size of government, which would be beneficial for economic growth in the long term. Critics were concerned that the cuts would slow down an already precarious economic recovery and cost the nation approximately seven hundred thousand jobs.

The origins of the sequester can be traced to August 2011, when President Barack Obama and the Republicans in Congress were at loggerheads over raising the debt ceiling, also known as the federal debt limit, which is the amount of money the federal government can borrow to pay its bills. In order to raise the debt ceiling, Congress had to pass a debt ceiling increase.

While the Democrats argued that raising the debt ceiling should be a matter of normal business, Republicans refused to raise it without major spending cuts. When negotiations over a "grand bargain" on the debt ceiling broke down, Republicans proposed the creation of the Joint Select Committee on Deficit Reduction, also known as the Supercommittee, to negotiate substantial budget cuts down the road. If the bipartisan committee could not reach an agreement to cut around $1.5 trillion from the federal budget, then the automatic sequestration would kick in on January 1, 2013. The prospect of across-the-board cuts to defense and domestic programs were regarded as a strong incentive for both parties to come together and find a solution to the budget impasse. Both Republicans and Democrats wanted some say as to which programs and departments would be most impacted by spending cuts, and neither party wanted to admit that Congress was too dysfunctional to come to a deal on something so integral to the economic recovery and the nation's overall economic health.

It was clear by late 2012 that Congress was indeed ineffective in compromising. With no deal in sight, the sequester was postponed until March 1, 2013. The day before the deadline, President Obama derided Congress's inability to come to a compromise and predicted that the sequestration cuts could have major economic consequences. "[These] cuts are not smart," he observed. "They are not fair. They will hurt our economy. . . . And that's why Democrats, Republicans, business leaders, and economists, they've already said that these cuts, known here in Washington as sequestration, are a bad idea. They're not good for our economy. That's not how we should run our government. And here's the thing: They don't have to happen. There is a smarter way to do this—to reduce our deficits without harming our economy. But Congress has to act in order for that to happen."

Sequestration is just one recent example of the dysfunction that affects America's economic health and national security. There are others discussed in this chapter, which debates the scope and implications of government gridlock.

"*[With] this endless parade of distractions and political posturing and phony scandals, Washington has taken its eye off the ball. And I am here to say this needs to stop.*"

Government Gridlock Is a Major Impediment to Solving America's Problems

Barack Obama

Barack Obama is the forty-fourth president of the United States. In the following viewpoint, he outlines the serious economic and political challenges faced by the United States today and claims that government gridlock has been a formidable obstacle in effectively confronting those problems. Obama focuses on the issue of income inequality, in which almost all of the economic gains of the past several years have largely benefited only the top 1 percent of Americans. To maintain a fair and vibrant economy, he contends that all Americans must benefit from economic growth. He asserts that economic inequality should be Congress's top priority. Obama challenges congressional Republicans to lay out a positive agenda and proposes both parties find common ground to help America's middle class.

Barack Obama, "Remarks on the US Economy," Whitehouse.gov, July 24, 2013.

As you read, consider the following questions:

1. According to Obama, how much did the income of the top 1 percent increase from 1979 to 2007?

2. How many new jobs does President Obama say were created in the United States over the past forty months?

3. What great American writer does Obama identify as being born in Galesburg, Illinois, the site of this speech on the economy?

In the period after World War II, a growing middle class was the engine of our prosperity. Whether you owned a company, or swept its floors, or worked anywhere in between, this country offered you a basic bargain—a sense that your hard work would be rewarded with fair wages and decent benefits, the chance to buy a home, to save for retirement, and most of all, a chance to hand down a better life for your kids.

But over time, that engine began to stall—and a lot of folks here saw it—that bargain began to fray. Technology made some jobs obsolete. Global competition sent a lot of jobs overseas. It became harder for unions to fight for the middle class. Washington doled out bigger tax cuts to the very wealthy and smaller minimum wage increases for the working poor.

And so what happened was that the link between higher productivity and people's wages and salaries was broken. It used to be that, as companies did better, as profits went higher, workers also got a better deal. And that started changing. So the income of the top 1 percent nearly quadrupled from 1979 to 2007, but the typical family's income barely budged.

And toward the end of those three decades, a housing bubble, credit cards, a churning financial sector was keeping the economy artificially juiced up, so sometimes it papered over some of these long-term trends. But by the time I took office in 2009 as your president, we all know the bubble had burst, and it cost millions of Americans their jobs, and their homes, and their savings. And I know a lot of folks in this area were hurt pretty bad. And the decades-long erosion that had been taking place—the erosion of middle-class security—was suddenly laid bare for everybody to see.

The American Comeback

Now, today, five years after the start of that Great Recession, America has fought its way back. We fought our way back. Together, we saved the auto industry; took on a broken health care system. We invested in new American technologies to reverse our addiction to foreign oil. We doubled wind and solar power. Together, we put in place tough new rules on the big banks and protections to crack down on the worst practices of mortgage lenders and credit card companies. We changed a tax code too skewed in favor of the wealthiest at the expense of working families—so we changed that, and we locked in tax cuts for 98 percent of Americans, and we asked those at the top to pay a little bit more.

So you add it all up, and over the past 40 months, our businesses have created 7.2 million new jobs. This year [2013], we're off to our strongest private sector job growth since 1999.

And because we bet on this country, suddenly foreign companies are, too. Right now, more of Honda's cars are made in America than anyplace else on Earth. Airbus, the European aircraft company, they're building new planes in Alabama. And American companies like Ford are replacing outsourcing with insourcing—they're bringing jobs back home.

We sell more products made in America to the rest of the world than ever before. We produce more natural gas than any country on Earth. We're about to produce more of our own oil than we buy from abroad for the first time in nearly 20 years. The cost of health care is growing at its slowest rate in 50 years. And our deficits are falling at the fastest rate in 60 years.

So thanks to the grit and resilience and determination of the American people—of folks like you—we've been able to clear away the rubble from the financial crisis. We started to lay a new foundation for stronger, more durable economic growth. And it's happening in our own personal lives as well, right? A lot of us tightened our belts, shed debt, maybe cut up a couple of credit cards, refocused on those things that really matter.

As a country, we've recovered faster and gone further than most other advanced nations in the world. With new American revolutions in energy and technology and manufacturing and health care, we're actually poised to reverse the forces that battered the middle class for so long and start building an economy where everyone who works hard can get ahead.

More Work to Do

But—and here's the big "but"—I'm here to tell you today that we're not there yet. We all know that. We're not there yet. We've got more work to do. Even though our businesses are creating new jobs and have broken record profits, nearly all the income gains of the past 10 years have continued to flow to the top 1 percent. The average CEO [chief executive officer] has gotten a raise of nearly 40 percent since 2009. The average American earns less than he or she did in 1999. And companies continue to hold back on hiring those who've been out of work for some time.

Today, more students are earning their degree, but soaring costs saddle them with unsustainable debt. Health care costs are slowing down, but a lot of working families haven't seen any of those savings yet. The stock market rebound helped a lot of families get back much of what they had lost in their 401(k)s, but millions of Americans still have no idea how they're going to be able to retire.

So in many ways, the trends that I spoke about here in 2005—eight years ago—the trend of a winner-take-all economy where a few are doing better and better and better, while everybody else just treads water—those trends have been made worse by the recession. And that's a problem. . . .

This growing inequality is not just morally wrong, it's bad economics. Because when middle-class families have less to spend, guess what, businesses have fewer consumers. When wealth concentrates at the very top, it can inflate unstable bubbles that threaten the economy. When the rungs on the ladder of opportunity grow farther and farther apart, it undermines the very essence of America—that idea that if you work hard you can make it here.

And that's why reversing these trends has to be Washington's highest priority. It has to be Washington's highest priority. It's certainly my highest priority.

The Problem with Gridlock

Unfortunately, over the past couple of years, in particular, Washington hasn't just ignored this problem; too often, Washington has made things worse.

And I have to say that—because I'm looking around the room—I've got some friends here not just who are Democrats, I've got some friends here who are Republicans—and I worked with in the state legislature and they did great work. But right now, what we've got in Washington, we've seen a sizable group of Republican lawmakers suggest that they wouldn't vote to pay the very bills that Congress rang up. And that fiasco harmed a fragile recovery in 2011 and we can't afford to repeat that.

Then, rather than reduce our deficits with a scalpel—by cutting out programs we don't need, fixing ones that we do need that maybe are in need of reform, making government more efficient—instead of doing that, we've got folks who've insisted on leaving in place a meat cleaver called the sequester [general reduction of government spending] that's cost jobs.

It's harmed growth. It's hurt our military. It's gutted investments in education and science and medical research.

Almost every credible economist will tell you it's been a huge drag on this recovery. And it means that we're underinvesting in the things that this country needs to make it a magnet for good jobs.

Signs of Hope

Then, over the last six months, this gridlock has gotten worse. I didn't think that was possible. The good news is a growing number of Republican senators are looking to join their Democratic counterparts and try to get things done in the Senate. So that's good news. For example, they worked together on an immigration bill that economists say will boost our economy by more than a trillion dollars, strengthen border security, make the system work.

But you've got a faction of Republicans in the House who won't even give that bill a vote. And that same group gutted a farm bill that America's farmers depend on, but also America's most vulnerable children depend on. . . .

And if you ask some of these folks, some of these folks mostly in the House, about their economic agenda how it is that they'll strengthen the middle class, they'll shift the topic to "out-of-control government spending"—despite the fact that we've cut the deficit by nearly half as a share of the economy since I took office.

Or they'll talk about government assistance for the poor, despite the fact that they've already cut early education for vulnerable kids. They've already cut insurance for people who've lost their jobs through no fault of their own. Or they'll bring up Obamacare [referring to the Patient Protection and Affordable Care Act]—this is tried and true—despite the fact that our businesses have created nearly twice as many jobs in this recovery as businesses had at the same point in the last recovery when there was no Obamacare. . . .

President Barack Obama

Barack H. Obama is the 44th president of the United States.

His story is the American story—values from the heartland, a middle-class upbringing in a strong family, hard work and education as the means of getting ahead, and the conviction that a life so blessed should be lived in service to others. . . .

After working his way through college with the help of scholarships and student loans, President Obama moved to Chicago, where he worked with a group of churches to help rebuild communities devastated by the closure of local steel plants.

He went on to attend law school, where he became the first African-American president of the *Harvard Law Review*. Upon graduation, he returned to Chicago to help lead a voter registration drive, teach constitutional law at the University of Chicago, and remain active in his community. . . .

In the Illinois state senate, he passed the first major ethics reform in 25 years, cut taxes for working families, and expanded health care for children and their parents. As a United States senator, he reached across the aisle to pass groundbreaking lobbying reform, lock up the world's most dangerous weapons, and bring transparency to government by putting federal spending online.

"President Barack Obama," Whitehouse.gov, 2014.

But with this endless parade of distractions and political posturing and phony scandals, Washington has taken its eye off the ball. And I am here to say this needs to stop. This needs to stop.

Finding the Right Focus

This moment does not require short-term thinking. It does not require having the same old stale debates. Our focus has to be on the basic economic issues that matter most to you, the people we represent. That's what we have to spend our time on and our energy on and our focus on.

And as Washington prepares to enter another budget debate, the stakes for our middle class and everybody who is fighting to get into the middle class could not be higher. The countries that are passive in the face of a global economy, those countries will lose the competition for good jobs. They will lose the competition for high living standards. That's why America has to make the investments necessary to promote long-term growth and shared prosperity—rebuilding our manufacturing base, educating our workforce, upgrading our transportation systems, upgrading our information networks. That's what we need to be talking about. That's what Washington needs to be focused on.

And that's why, over the next several weeks, in towns across this country, I will be engaging the American people in this debate. I'll lay out my ideas for how we build on the cornerstones of what it means to be middle class in America, and what it takes to work your way into the middle class in America: Job security, with good wages and durable industries. A good education. A home to call your own. Affordable health care when you get sick. A secure retirement even if you're not rich. Reducing poverty. Reducing inequality. Growing opportunity. That's what we need. That's what we need. That's what we need right now. That's what we need to be focused on. . . .

A Positive Agenda

It's interesting, in the run-up to this speech, a lot of reporters say that, well, Mr. President, these are all good ideas, but some of you've said before; some of them sound great, but you can't get those through Congress. Republicans won't agree with you. And I say, look, the fact is there are Republicans in Congress right now who privately agree with me on a lot of the ideas I'll be proposing. I know because they've said so. But they worry they'll face swift political retaliation for cooperating with me.

Now, there are others who will dismiss every idea I put forward either because they're playing to their most strident supporters, or in some cases because, sincerely, they have a fundamentally different vision for America—one that says inequality is both inevitable and just; one that says an unfettered free market without any restraints inevitably produces the best outcomes, regardless of the pain and uncertainty imposed on ordinary families; and government is the problem and we should just shrink it as small as we can.

In either case, I say to these members of Congress: I'm laying out my ideas to give the middle class a better shot. So now it's time for you to lay out your ideas. You can't just be against something. You got to be for something.

Even if you think I've done everything wrong, the trends I just talked about were happening well before I took office. So it's not enough for you just to oppose me. You got to be for something. What are your ideas? If you're willing to work with me to strengthen American manufacturing and rebuild this country's infrastructure, let's go. If you've got better ideas to bring down the cost of college for working families, let's hear them. If you think you have a better plan for making sure that every American has the security of quality, affordable health care, then stop taking meaningless repeal votes, and share your concrete ideas with the country.

Repealing Obamacare and cutting spending is not an economic plan. It's not.

If you're serious about a balanced, long-term fiscal plan that replaces the mindless cuts currently in place, or if you're interested in tax reform that closes corporate loopholes and gives working families a better deal, I'm ready to work. But you should know that I will not accept deals that don't meet the basic test of strengthening the prospects of hardworking families. This is the agenda we have to be working on.

The Danger of Inaction

We've come a long way since I first took office. As a country, we're older and wiser. I don't know if I'm wiser, but I'm certainly older. And as long as Congress doesn't manufacture another crisis—as long as we don't shut down the government just because I'm for keeping it open—as long as we don't risk a U.S. default over paying bills that we've already racked up, something that we've never done—we can probably muddle along without taking bold action. If we stand pat and we don't do any of the things I talked about, our economy will grow, although slower than it should. New businesses will form. The unemployment rate will probably tick down a little bit. Just by virtue of our size and our natural resources and, most of all, because of the talent of our people, America will remain a world power, and the majority of us will figure out how to get by.

But you know what, that's our choice. If we just stand by and do nothing in the face of immense change, understand that part of our character will be lost. Our founding precepts about wide-open opportunity, each generation doing better than the last—that will be a myth, not reality. The position of the middle class will erode further. Inequality will continue to increase. Money's power will distort our politics even more.

Social tensions will rise, as various groups fight to hold on to what they have, or start blaming somebody else for why their position isn't improving. And the fundamental optimism that's always propelled us forward will give way to cynicism or nostalgia.

And that's not the vision I have for this country. It's not the vision you have for this country. That's not the America we know. That's not the vision we should be settling for. That's not a vision we should be passing on to our children.

Helping Working Americans

I have now run my last campaign. I do not intend to wait until the next campaign or the next president before tackling the issues that matter. I care about one thing and one thing only, and that's how to use every minute—the only thing I care about is how to use every minute of the remaining 1,276 days of my term—to make this country work for working Americans again. That's all I care about. I don't have another election.

Because I'll tell you, Galesburg, [Illinois,] that's where I believe America needs to go. I believe that's where the American people want to go. And it may seem hard today, but if we're willing to take a few bold steps—if Washington will just shake off its complacency and set aside the kind of slash-and-burn partisanship that we've just seen for way too long—if we just make some commonsense decisions, our economy will be stronger a year from now. It will be stronger five years from now. It will be stronger 10 years from now.

If we focus on what matters, then more Americans will know the pride of that first paycheck. More Americans will have the satisfaction of flipping the sign to "Open" on their own business. More Americans will have the joy of scratching the height of their kid on that door of their brand-new home.

America's Unique Qualities

And in the end, isn't that what makes us special? It's not the ability to generate incredible wealth for the few; it's our ability to give everybody a chance to pursue their own true measure of happiness. We haven't just wanted success for ourselves—we want it for our neighbors, too.

When we think about our own communities—we're not a mean people; we're not a selfish people; we're not a people that just looks out for "number one." Why should our politics reflect those kinds of values? That's why we don't call it John's dream or Susie's dream or Barack's dream or Pat's dream—we call it the American dream. And that's what makes this country special; the idea that no matter who you are or what you look like or where you come from or who you love, you can make it if you try. That's what we're fighting for.

So, yes, Congress is tough right now, but that's not going to stop me. We're going to do everything we can, wherever we can, with or without Congress, to make things happen. We're going to go on the road and talk to you, and you'll have ideas, and we want to see which ones we can implement. But we're going to focus on this thing that matters.

One of America's greatest writers, Carl Sandburg, born right here in Galesburg over a century ago, he saw the railroads bring the world to the prairie, and then the prairie sent out its bounty to the world. And he saw the advent of new industries, new technologies, and he watched populations shift. He saw fortunes made and lost. And he saw how change could be painful—how a new age could unsettle long-held customs and ways of life. But he had that frontier optimism, and so he saw something more on the horizon. And he wrote, "I speak of new cities and new people. The past is a bucket of ashes. Yesterday is a wind gone down, a sun dropped in the west. There is only an ocean of tomorrows, a sky of tomorrows."

Well, America, we've made it through the worst of yesterday's winds. We just have to have the courage to keep moving forward. We've got to set our eyes on the horizon. We will find an ocean of tomorrows. We will find a sky of tomorrows for the American people and for this great country that we love.

> *"That's what checks and balances are supposed to do: prevent precipitous action and sometimes guarantee no action at all."*

Congressional Gridlock Is Good

Russell E. Saltzman

Russell E. Saltzman is a political analyst and contributor to First Things. *In the following viewpoint, he rejects the idea of government gridlock as catastrophic. In fact, Saltzman asserts, gridlock has a number of major benefits, including the ability to stop ill-advised and impetuous legislation. He asserts that gridlock was an integral part of the original framework of the US Constitution, and the creation of a two-chamber legislature ensures that there would always be an internal check on both houses of Congress. Saltzman points out that throughout American history there have been Congresses that have been gridlocked and that still managed to pass major legislation and confront serious problems. The key, he argues, is that they knew how to negotiate—a skill that the current Congress does not have.*

As you read, consider the following questions:

1. What prominent American politician does Saltzman identify as responsible for government gridlock?

2. According to the author, how many Congresses have been party gridlocked since the very first Congress?

3. How many American presidents does the author cite as having enjoyed all their presidential years with their party in control of both houses?

The complaints and worry and agonizing anxiousness about the fiscal cliff and Washington gridlock have an alarming air of coming apocalypse. Phrases wafting around include but are not limited to "divided dysfunctional government," "the worst Congress ever," and "the grip of partisan gridlock."

The mixed election results, "call them a political mulligan," have, many argue, set us up for more of the same horrible things we have endured since the 2010 congressional elections: Two congressional houses split between competing parties and, consequently, a government where nothing gets done.

The House of Representatives is controlled by a party opposed to the president while the Senate is pro-administration. Republicans and Democrats are locked up in a bottle like ideological scorpions. A gridlocked government is bad, bad, bad, and we must do something to "get this country moving again."

Naturally this is all the fault of hyper-partisan principals in Congress who have lost their knowledge, if they ever had it, of the art of compromise. (Let me add, in the interest of high bipartisanship, that the White House doesn't seem to know much about it either.)

But there are major benefits to gridlock. I'm a "stop and smell the roses" political sort of guy. Especially if they are government roses, I want to know how much it will cost to cultivate them. Really, I'd happily settle for marigolds. I like that legislation is supposed to go along in a deliberately slow-motion process. The trouble seems to come from fast-tracked legislative impetuousness, and even no legislation is still a legislative decision. That's what checks and balances are supposed to do: prevent precipitous action and sometimes guarantee no action at all. That is how we set it up.

We may lay the praise or the blame for that at the feet of James Madison. His Virginia Plan at the 1787 Constitutional Convention was the original framework, with some compromise, for what became the U.S. Constitution. The convention created a two-chamber legislature, ensuring each served as a break on the other, and the later party system ensured a further internal check. There is always somebody watching.

Along with a list of comprehensive congressional powers, the convention gave some exclusive fiscal power to the House and some exclusive power in foreign relations to the Senate, yet both must agree to legislation resulting from those exclusive powers. Add an executive with a veto over acts of the legislature (which also enjoys the power of executive impeachment), create an independent judiciary that can and has overturned decisions of both Congress and the president and woohoo! Gridlock. It's part of our constitutional DNA.

This isn't the first Congress to be gridlocked. In the early years of Congress there were no party labels, but that doesn't mean parties didn't exist. From the very first Congress (1789–1791), Federalists ("pro-administration") and Anti-Federalists ("anti-administration") vied against each other. By the third Congress (1793–1795), we are talking gridlock. Congress had a "pro-administration" Senate and an "anti-administration" House. Of 112 Congresses (the one hundred thirteenth has yet to be seated), twenty-one have been party gridlocked.

Twenty-two of our forty-four presidents served during times when one house of Congress was dominated for at least some portion of the presidential tenure by a party in opposition to the president's own.

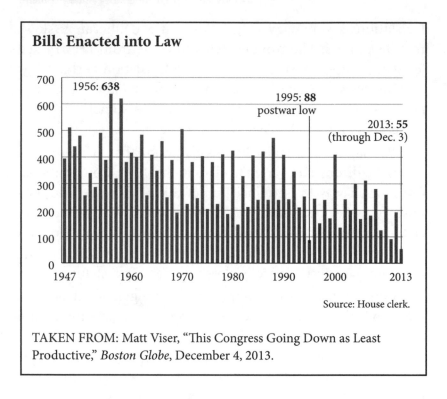

Bills Enacted into Law

1956: **638**

1995: **88**
postwar low

2013: **55**
(through Dec. 3)

Source: House clerk.

TAKEN FROM: Matt Viser, "This Congress Going Down as Least Productive," *Boston Globe*, December 4, 2013.

That does not count the six presidents whose party was a congressional minority in both houses throughout their entire term. And only fifteen presidents have enjoyed all their presidential years with their party in control of both houses.

George Washington, John Quincy Adams, Andrew Jackson, Grover Cleveland (both times), and Woodrow Wilson, among others, all faced a divided Congress. We've had twenty presidents since 1900; nine in total have been confronted with a divided Congress and, beginning with Ronald Reagan, every president since (except George H.W. Bush, whose party was in the minority his entire term).

Gridlocks appear to come in clusters: 1789–1797, two of four gridlocked; 1824–1861, six of seventeen gridlocked; 1875–1883, three of four gridlocked; 1887–1931, five of twenty-two; 1981–2013, five of sixteen.

For many periods in our national history, congressional gridlock has been a default setting. Yet from these Congresses has come an array of significant legislative acts. A gridlocked Congress admitted Texas to the Union on a joint resolution by the House and Senate, the first federal revenue sharing act was adopted by a gridlocked Congress, and the same Congress adopted the income tax.

Best I can see it, and this is my judgment call, a gridlocked Congress is never entirely a do-nothing Congress. Much of what Congress may or may not accomplish is a result of presidential leadership, flexibility, and his ability to charm Congress. There the record is plainly mixed, pretty much as it is with a Congress that isn't gridlocked.

> *"This clash over the proper role for gov-*
> *ernment in the US is one that has de-*
> *fined our national politics for more*
> *than a century."*

Government Gridlock Reflects an Increasingly Dysfunctional Political System

Michael A. Cohen

Michael A. Cohen is an author, political commentator, and fellow at the Century Foundation. In the following viewpoint, he suggests that the government gridlock paralyzing US politics today reflects a political system that seems incapable of confronting the nation's problems. Cohen views the two-party system as central to the country's dysfunction. One party, the Democrats, perceives government as an effective force for good in the lives of all Americans; the other, the Republicans, wants to shrink the role of government and lessen its control over business and individuals. Cohen says that as the Republican Party has become more ideological and less willing to compromise, the ability of government to deal with serious challenges has diminished. In turn, public confidence in the government has plummeted.

As you read, consider the following questions:

1. According to Cohen, what prominent American president did Barack Obama quote in his election speech in 2008?

2. According to the viewpoint, what ratings agency downgraded US debt in 2011?

3. What does the Fourteenth Amendment of the US Constitution call for, according to the author?

Nearly three years ago [in November of 2008], on a night of great history, a slender 47-year-old black man who had just been elected to the nation's highest political office offered the American people an optimistic vision for the country's future. Quoting Abraham Lincoln, Barack Obama spoke of national unity: "We are not enemies, but friends. Though passion may have strained, it must not break our bonds of affection."

That night, Obama offered the American people a clear sense of his overriding priority as president—it wasn't just to fix the ailing US economy, provide health care for all or end the war in Iraq. But rather, after eight years of political turmoil and disunity, through the force of his personality and political temperament, Obama would, as Lincoln said, "bind up the nation's wounds."

A Well-Laid Plan

Things have not quite worked out as Obama planned. Even with poll results suggesting that Americans prize compromise and are tired of overt partisanship, the level of division and acrimony in Washington has grown exponentially since Obama took office. The recent debt limit debate is the apogee of Washington's dysfunction and indicative of a political system that is seemingly incapable of dealing with national challenges. Indeed, whatever one may think of Standard & Poor's recent downgrade of US debt, the ratings agency's view that "the effectiveness, stability, and predictability of American policymaking and political institutions have weakened" seems almost self-evident.

A Dire Situation

How has America been reduced to one party holding a gun to the US economy and the other trading away its political principles to stop the trigger from being pulled? The problem is that the US today has one party intent on utilising government resources as a force for social good and another that rejects any significant role for the public sector. Compounding this collision of ideologies is a populace so indifferent to the workings of their own government that they are unable to choose which model they prefer.

This clash over the proper role for government in the US is one that has defined our national politics for more than a century. But in the last several years this conflict has become an existential one, with Republicans basically abdicating their responsibility to govern. When in power, they made little effort to deal with the nation's many challenges. In opposition, and particularly in the two and a half years since Obama took office, they have used the tool of the Senate filibuster and various other procedural impediments to try to stop nearly all Democratic initiatives in their tracks. Whatever legislation passed in the past few years is almost solely a product of Democratic cohesion (an attribute that is generally in short supply)—and a brief window in which Democrats enjoyed a filibuster-proof majority in the US Senate.

Scorched-Earth Politics

From this perspective, threatening economic cataclysm in order to further reduce the size of government, by refusing to raise the debt limit, now seems like an inevitable step in Washington's scorched-earth politics. That it forced Democrats to agree to trillions in painful spending cuts without any commensurate revenue hikes shows how successful this strategy of policy extortion can be.

So why do Democrats put up with it? They have little choice. The American political system discourages radicalism and relies on compromise. Yet the violation of even the most customary rules of governance has made such deal making now nearly impossible. It was once considered a given that, with the rarest of exceptions, a president would be able to appoint his own charges to key policy-making positions; and the debt ceiling was considered an occasionally politicised but generally pro forma exercise. No longer. In a system designed around collegiality, Democrats have few tools in their arsenal to combat the GOP's political obstinacy.

As a result, America is increasingly moving toward a parliamentary system in which politicians, rather than voting along regional lines or in pursuit of parochial interests, cast their ballot solely based on whether there is a D or R next to their name. Such a system might work well in the UK [United Kingdom], but in the US, with its institutional focus on checks and balances and the many tools available for stopping legislation, a parliamentary-style system is a recipe for inaction.

Protecting the Government

What compounds the Democrats' challenge is that they are the party of activist government. When in opposition, they find it hard to use the Republicans' jamming techniques; when in power they feel the almost quaint need to act responsibly. Any scent of scandal or illegitimate behaviour that undermines the electorate's confidence in government in turn undermines the Democrat's brand.

Case in point on the debt: Liberals far and wide urged Obama to consider invoking the 14th Amendment of the US Constitution, which suggests that the country's public debt must continue to be paid. As the Left argued, this would have

"THE REASON THE COST OF GOVERNMENT IS SO HIGH IS THAT IT TAKES HUNDREDS OF CONGRESSMEN LOCKED IN A ROOM TO PRODUCE GRIDLOCK."

© Harley Schwadron/CartoonStock.com.

resolved the crisis. In a worst-case scenario, Republicans might impeach the president in the House of Representatives, but, as the argument went, wouldn't this be a good way to rally the country around Obama? But such tactical recommendations miss a crucial element; if low-information voters (the vast majority of Americans) look to Washington and see the nation's political leaders arguing about impeachment and constitutional crises that have little connection to their own lives, it exacerbates their lack of confidence in government. For many conservatives, it would only confirm their irrational belief that President Obama is a power-hungry tyrant.

Political Aspects

Thus for Democrats, gridlock is their most pernicious enemy; a point Republicans understand all too well. The more they stop government from operating effectively, the more it emphasises their key political narrative that there is no reason to have any confidence in public institutions. Tom Schaller, a political scientist at the University of Maryland, said to me that Republicans understand that if you have a vat of sewage and you pour in a glass of wine you still have a vat of sewage. But if you pour a glass of sewage into a vat of wine, guess what, you now have a vat of sewage. In short, a little political poison can go a long way. So while liberal complaints that President Obama is far too solicitous of Republicans and far too wedded to his post-partisan agenda (all probably true), a reversion to bare-knuckled politics is not necessarily going to make things any easier or better for progressives.

As the Democratic pollster Stanley Greenberg noted in the *New York Times*, "voters feel ever more estranged from government" and "they associate Democrats with government". More crises in Washington are not going to help that process.

Why do voters put up with such a situation? Polling suggests that the electorate wants their leaders to focus on jobs, rather than the deficit; and work toward compromise, rather than gridlock. So why then do they reward political parties, such as the Republicans, that act decidedly against not only their preferences but also their interests?

Voter Apathy

The answer lies in the apathy of the American people toward their own government. The ultimate check on Republican nihilism would be voter revolt. But in the last congressional election, voters rewarded unprecedented Republican obstructionism with control of the House of Representatives.

What's worse, voter preferences are often contradictory. Polls suggest that the electorate wants political leaders to cut spending, but then also demand no cuts in any government programme that isn't foreign aid. They want Congress to focus more on creating jobs, but recoil at policies, such as the bailout of the US auto industry or the stimulus package, that did just that. One problem is that Americans have been so inundated with antigovernment rhetoric over the past 40 years they seem to have trouble identifying any link between government engagement and a robust economy.

Worst of all, Americans may prefer Democratic policies, but they have little confidence in government's ability to fulfil those promises and then blame both parties for inaction. They are so mistrustful of government and shockingly uninformed about its working that, perversely, via the ballot boxes, they directly contribute to the political stalemate they so regularly decry.

The Result

The result is a political system that is perhaps more incapacitated than at any point in modern history. Across the US, states have to cut social services and benefits because they are receiving no support from the federal government. Infrastructure is crumbling, millions of American students are trapped in underperforming schools, the existential threat of climate change is off the political radar screen and job growth is barely on the agenda. Even the most recent agreement to cut the bloated federal deficit does virtually nothing to deal with the greatest driver of national indebtedness—health care spending. What all of this suggests is that the episode played out over the past few weeks of one party threatening to plunge the nation into economic catastrophe is not some rare event—it's the new norm in American politics. And perhaps the most glaring indication that Barack Obama's vision of new post-partisan America will be a dream perhaps permanently deferred.

> "A return to the frustrating, sluggish, gridlock-prone system of legislation set forth in the Constitution will actually enhance representation of broad, unorganized, public interests."

The Case for Gridlock

Marcus E. Ethridge

Marcus E. Ethridge is a professor of political science at the University of Wisconsin–Madison and the author of The Case for Gridlock: Democracy, Organized Power, and the Legal Foundations of American Government. *In the following viewpoint, he argues that government gridlock benefits the economically and socially disadvantaged because it stifles the efforts of narrow, organized groups in favor of broad, unorganized groups. Ethridge acknowledges that lessening economic inequality is a top priority for Progressive politicians, but he says that efforts to avoid congressional gridlock by delegating power to administrative agencies and issuing executive orders only exacerbates inequality by rewarding the efforts of well-organized groups with narrow interests. Evidence shows, he claims, that collective efforts in support of Progressive causes, such as addressing economic inequality, have been historically ineffective.*

As you read, consider the following questions:

1. According to one expert, what will be the result of the Dodd-Frank financial reform legislation?

2. What does Ethridge claim James MacGregor Burns's book *The Deadlock of Democracy* is about?

3. What was the title of Mancur Olson Jr.'s landmark book, which was published in 1965?

In the wake of the 2010 elections, President [Barack] Obama declared that voters did not give a mandate to gridlock. His statement reflects over a century of Progressive hostility to the inefficient and slow system of government created by the American framers. Convinced that the government created by the Constitution frustrates their goals, Progressives have long sought ways around its checks and balances. Perhaps the most important of their methods is delegating power to administrative agencies, an arrangement that greatly transformed U.S. government during and after the New Deal. For generations, Progressives have supported the false premise that administrative action in the hands of experts will realize the public interest more effectively than the constitutional system and its multiple vetoes over policy changes. The political effect of empowering the administrative state has been quite different: It fosters policies that reflect the interests of those with well-organized power. A large and growing body of evidence makes it clear that the public interest is most secure when governmental institutions are inefficient decision makers. An arrangement that brings diverse interests into a complex, sluggish decision-making process is generally unattractive to special interests. Gridlock also neutralizes some political benefits that producer groups and other well-heeled interests inherently enjoy. By fostering gridlock, the U.S. Constitution increases the likelihood that policies will reflect broad, unorganized interests instead of the interests of narrow, organized groups.

Introduction

It has been clear for some time now that the second half of President Obama's first term will be marked by deep gridlock. Given the composition of the 112th Congress, passing major legislation will be very difficult. However, while the congressional-presidential system is in gridlock, a great deal of energetic lawmaking will take place *outside* the constitutional system. By continuing—and expanding—the delegation of legislative power to "unicameral" executive agencies, the Obama administration and its allies in Congress will use a highly efficient way to make policy. The contrast between these two processes for producing legislation will give us an excellent opportunity to appreciate the virtues of the protracted, frustrating institutional arrangement set forth by the framers.

According to one expert, the Dodd-Frank [Wall Street Reform and Consumer Protection Act] will lead to at least 243 separate instances of administrative rule making, involving nine different agencies and commissions. The Obama administration has already used administrative "legislation" to make policy on offshore oil drilling, stem cell research, and a variety of environmental issues. And the Department of Health and Human Services has granted more than 200 waivers from key provisions of the new health care reform. In deeply important ways, non-elected officials are making the public's policies.

Ever since the time of Woodrow Wilson, Progressives have argued that policy making by expert executive agencies is far superior to the "antique" legislative process crafted by the Constitution's framers. Just as they argued a century ago, modern Progressives contend that moving legislative authority outside the congressional-presidential system will lead to more efficient and informed policy making. But they also argue that, by circumventing the gridlock-prone institutional arrangement, policies that advance social equality and progress will no longer be obstructed by commercial interests. Reducing the role of gridlock-prone institutions will thus lead to a more just and progressive society.

However, the Progressive vision is profoundly wrong. Decades of experience and research on interest groups and the workings of administrative policy making clearly demonstrate that the more efficiently responsive the government is, the greater the influence of interests that enjoy the political advantages of superior organization. A return to the frustrating, sluggish, gridlock-prone system of legislation set forth in the Constitution will actually enhance representation of broad, unorganized, public interests.

Progressivism and Gridlock

In 2006, Nobel laureate Paul Krugman spoke for many politicians and academics, including several who would become influential members of the Obama administration, when he offered this assessment of contemporary U.S. inequality: "It is not hard to foresee, in the current state of our political and economic scene, the outline of a transformation into a permanently unequal society—one that locks in and perpetuates the drastic economic polarization that is already dangerously far advanced." Krugman's complaint was remarkably consistent with the views of Progressive commentators from previous generations. Theodore Roosevelt [TR] argued that big business was a special interest that enjoyed disproportionate power. A quarter-century later, Franklin Roosevelt [FDR] remarked: "For too many of us the political equality we once had was meaningless in the face of economic inequality."

Equality, depending on the way it is measured, has varied considerably over the last century. But the Progressive argument that (a) inequality has reached intolerable levels, and (b) the political power of wealthy interests obstructs efforts to reduce it, has remained unchanged for generations.

The persistence of the Progressive complaint about social and economic equality is perplexing in light of the policies and programs that were adopted between the time of Teddy Roosevelt and Paul Krugman. In the decades between 1910 and today, U.S. society experienced the imposition of and massive expansion of the income tax, extensive government regulation of the private sector, and a series of entitlement programs enacted during the New Deal and the Great Society eras that now account for most of a very large government budget. If a time machine could bring TR to the present, he would doubtlessly be stunned to find contemporary commentators writing bitterly about "savage inequalities" and a "permanent lower class" after the successful adoption of so many landmark Progressive initiatives.

How can such inequalities persist after so many Progressive programs were implemented? The answer is not simply that Progressive policies have unintended consequences or that they are based on flawed ideas about economics (although such criticisms are frequently on target). The deeper problem is that the institutional changes made to craft and implement these policies increased the political power of the well organized. Moving much of the legislative process to executive branch agencies certainly made lawmaking more efficient, but it also had political consequences that undermined Progressive goals. Contrary to heated statements from Progressives from TR to Krugman, the case for gridlock is the case for equality and the representation of broad interests.

A 1984 Supreme Court decision, astonishing in its frankness, provides a compelling illustration of the power of organized interests in efficiently responsive institutional settings. In *Block v. Community Nutrition Institute*, a group advocating for the interests of the poor challenged an Agriculture Department "milk-market order." For decades, agricultural interests had persuaded the department to use the statutory authority granted by Congress to raise milk prices, enriching them at the expense of consumers. The community group wanted the department to consider the effect of its action on consumers, especially the poor. Justice Sandra Day O'Connor rejected their claims as she wrote for a unanimous court:

> Congress intended that judicial review of market orders ordinarily be confined to suits by [dairy] handlers. . . . Allowing consumers to sue the Secretary would severely disrupt the Act's complex and delicate administrative scheme. . . . [T]he congressional intent to preclude consumer suits is "fairly discernible" in the detail of the legislative scheme. *The Act contemplates a cooperative venture among the Secretary, producers, and handlers; consumer participation is not provided for or desired under that scheme.*

This case not only reveals that interest-group power can influence policy, but it shows how it does so most effectively *in an efficient institutional context.* The Agriculture Department adopted its milk-market orders in a setting without bicameralism, without inter-institutional competition, and with the participation of a clearly targeted interest. Progressives strongly supported the expansion of the Agriculture Department's powers during the New Deal. But the efficient responsiveness that their reforms created frequently undercut Progressive policy goals.

A generation of research on the way organized interests influence government amply demonstrates that the gridlock-prone constitutional system obstructs "rent seeking" and other forms of influence by privileged political organizations far more than it obstructs influence by the unorganized. The tragedy of Progressivism is that, in its frustration with the existence of social and political inequality, it demands the establishment of institutions that amplify the political advantages of superior organization.

Progressivism's Claim That Institutional Efficiency Advances Social Equality

The idea that the Constitution's gridlock-prone institutions worsen social equality is a bedrock Progressive principle, made explicit in James Allen Smith's *The Spirit of American Government* in 1906. For Smith, Charles Beard, and other Progressives of their time, the constitutional arrangement of government institutions was a critical obstacle to progress. Later Progressives developed the idea. Following mid-century pluralists like David Truman, they accepted the idea that nearly all interests—including the poor, labor, consumers, and even taxpayers—can be represented by effective political organizations. Consequently, if the political system fails to achieve social equality, there must be something in the design of governmental institutions that stands in the way of progress. Progressive thinkers attributed this failure to the gridlock-prone institutional arrangement that the framers left us. Thus, most Progressives believe that it is not necessary to have a thoroughgoing revolution as Marxists and other radicals claimed—circumventing gridlock would naturally produce a more progressive and just society.

Some of the most cited political scientists of the century agreed. James MacGregor Burns's *The Deadlock of Democracy* (1963) expressed frustration with a system that had to be forcibly attacked by activist presidents to produce results: "Even the strongest and ablest presidents have been, in the end, more the victims of the Madisonian system than the masters of it." His criticism of institutional gridlock clearly embodied the Progressive view that, if only the archaic checks and balances were removed (or circumvented), majority interests would flourish. Similarly, in what became a mid-century classic of political science, Robert Dahl argued that "Madison's nicely contrived system of constitutional checks" prevented the poor from having "anything like equal control over government policy."

New Dealer James Landis argued that the frustrations and delays produced by the Madisonian system could be circumvented, an approach far easier than explicit constitutional change. In 1938, he wrote *The Administrative Process*, a book that legitimized much of what FDR had done, while laying the foundation for continued support for the Progressive way of thinking for subsequent generations:

> So much in the way of hope for the realization of claims to a better livelihood has, since the turn of the century, been made to rest upon the administrative process. To arm it with the means to effectuate those hopes is but to preserve the current of American living. . . . The administrative process springs from the inadequacy of a simple tripartite form of government to deal with modern problems. . . . [O]ur age must tolerate much more lightly the inefficiencies in the art of government.

Following this logic, Progressives worked successfully to change American institutions dramatically during the last century. The vast majority of laws are now made in unicameral administrative bodies, as Congress delegates many difficult decisions to agencies, and courts evolved a strong doctrine of deference to administrative judgments. The Progressive vision succeeded dramatically in creating a system in which government policy making could be more efficient than the antique system designed by the framers.

The Obama administration and its allies in Congress have fully embraced the Progressive approach. Even with strong Democratic majorities, it was difficult to enact the president's major legislative accomplishments (health care reform and the Dodd-Frank financial reform act). If the bills had included provisions that explicitly decided virtually all the major policy choices involved, their passage would not have been possible. Consequently, all of Obama's significant legislative successes provided for the *delegation* of legislative authority to a variety of executive branch commissions and agencies, sidestepping some of the difficult political decisions. Moving some important legislative tasks outside the gridlock-prone constitutional system made it possible to pass these landmark bills.

With a breathtaking disregard for the Constitution's first section ("All legislative Powers herein granted shall be vested in a Congress of the United States, which shall consist of a Senate and House of Representatives"), members of Congress were put on notice that if they failed to pass the administration's favored climate change legislation, the Environmental Protection Agency would resolve the issue by using its power to restrict carbon dioxide emissions as a "pollutant." It is a stunning demonstration of Progressivism's hold that so few citizens or commentators found this explicit assault on basic constitutional provisions noteworthy.

But Progressives have long contended that undermining or ignoring the legislative vesting clause is necessary in order to achieve progress and social equality. In large measure, the failure of Progressivism to achieve its goals is a function of Progressive delusions regarding how organized interests attempt to influence government. James Madison understood the problem quite well, and research by political scientists and economists has confirmed that his view remains more useful than the opposing arguments set out by Smith, Landis, and Krugman.

Why Progressive Institutions Fail

In 1965, Mancur Olson Jr. wrote a landmark book *(The Logic of Collective Action)* that provided a theoretical explanation for what many citizens and political insiders had long appreciated: Some interests are far more capable than others of producing effective organizations to advance their goals, and these fortunate interests are never the largest ones (they are not consumers, taxpayers, or the poor). If Olson is correct, the Progressive devotion to the administrative state cannot be reconciled with their concern for equality.

Olson argued that individuals will not normally contribute to a collective effort to advance their interests, even if those interests are important to them. Since a single contributor's effort and resources will have no real impact on the chances that the collective effort will be successful, and since non-contributors will receive benefits from any collective effort that is successful, the rational individual will not contribute. The most important implication of this idea (still largely unappreciated by Olson's numerous critics), is that there is no necessary correspondence between the array of political interests in society and the array of organized political forces working to influence government.

Several analysts have argued that the existence of organized political forces not anticipated by Olson undercuts his basic idea. The Sierra Club, the NAACP [National Association for the Advancement of Colored People], and NOW [National Organization for Women] are important political actors, even though they depend on voluntary collective action. While the mere founding of some of these organizations seems inconsistent with Olson's logic, such a criticism ignores the crucial point. When evaluating the distributive impact of institutional change, it is the relative political influence of competing interests that becomes critical. Even if we can identify a wide variety of political organizations that have somehow managed to exist and to set up lobbying operations in Washington, the free-rider problem suggests that groups will vary dramatically with respect to how much collective effort they get from those who share their collective interests: "More than 50 million Americans . . . value a wholesome environment, but in a typical year probably fewer than one in a hundred pays dues to any organization whose main activity is lobbying for a better environment. The proportion of physicians in the American Medical Association, or automobile workers in the United Automobile Workers union, or farmers in the Farm Bureau, or manufacturers in trade associations is incomparably greater." Olson's insight suggests that the array of organized lobbies active at any given time will *not* mirror the array of interests in society.

The critical issue for evaluating the Progressive position on the Constitution's lawmaking process is the extent to which the forces of organized political life, taken together, are democratically representative. Even if analysts are able to identify political organizations whose *existence* seems to challenge the validity of the free-rider problem, the conclusion that the *balance* of organized forces will not mirror the balance of political interests is unavoidable.

Periodical and Internet Sources Bibliography

The following articles have been selected to supplement the diverse views presented in this chapter.

Ralph Benko	"Bipartisanship Is Great for Politicians but Gridlock Is Better for the American People," *Forbes*, December 30, 2013.
Josh Boak	"Why Political Gridlock Could Sink the Economy," *Fiscal Times*, September 24, 2013.
Morris P. Fiorina	"Gridlock Is Bad. The Alternative Is Worse," *Washington Post*, February 25, 2014.
Danielle Kurtzleben	"Gridlock Just Might Be Good for the Economy," *U.S. News & World Report*, May 23, 2012.
Rick Lyman	"Governors Criticize Gridlock in Congress," *New York Times*, January 15, 2014.
Robert B. Reich	"The Real Price of Congress's Gridlock," *New York Times*, August 13, 2013.
Reihan Salam	"Josh Chafetz on 'The Phenomenology of Gridlock,'" *National Review Online*, January 21, 2013.
Betsey Stevenson	"How Government Gridlock Is Actively Hurting the Economy," *New Republic*, July 6, 2012.
John Stossel	"Three Cheers for Gridlock!," Fox News, November 14, 2012.
Adam B. Sullivan	"Leach Addresses Political Gridlock, Rising Inequality," *Des Moines Register* (Iowa), November 11, 2013.

OPPOSING
VIEWPOINTS®
SERIES

CHAPTER 2

What Are the Causes of Government Gridlock?

Chapter Preface

The Tea Party is a conservative populist political movement that gained traction in the wake of the 2008 economic crisis and the government bailout of America's financial and mortgage sectors. Many point to a rant from Rick Santelli, a financial reporter for the business-news network CNBC, as the official kickoff for the movement. On February 19, 2009, Santelli was reporting from the floor of the Chicago Board of Trade when he began to criticize the government's plan to spend an estimated $200 billion to refinance the mortgages of Americans.

"Why don't you put up a website to have people vote on the Internet as a referendum to see if we really want to subsidize the losers' mortgages," Santelli asked on CNBC, as traders around him began to cheer. "Or would we like to at least buy cars, buy a house that is in foreclosure . . . give it to people who might have a chance to actually prosper down the road and reward people that can carry the water instead of drink the water? This is America! How many of you people want to pay for your neighbor's mortgages that has an extra bathroom and can't pay their bills? . . . President Obama, are you listening? . . . It's time for another Tea Party!"

Santelli's rant became an Internet sensation. It was posted on numerous conservative sites and inspired many Americans to protest what they perceived to be the Barack Obama administration's profligate spending of billions of dollars of taxpayer money on government bailouts of big banks, the auto industry, and other Americans who had acted irresponsibly. By the next day, Tea Party groups were popping up all over the country and Fox News was enthusiastically referring to the Tea Party movement. On February 27, 2009, the first Tea Party protest was held in several cities across the country, attracting attention from mainstream media outlets. The Tea Party movement was officially launched.

The Tea Party is a decentralized movement, with no central hierarchal leadership, which leaves independent Tea Party groups to formulate their own agendas. These different Tea Party groups have a common goal: to cut government spending, shrink the size and scope of government, and bring down the federal deficit. Tea Party protests played a substantial role in opposing health care reform and the government bailout of the financial sector. However, some Tea Party groups have pushed traditional conservative social agendas, including anti-abortion laws, opposition to immigration reform and same-sex marriage, and gun advocacy. This has led to tension between some Tea Party groups, which want to avoid divisive social issues to attract a wide range of support, and other groups, which want to push a very narrow conservative agenda.

In the years following the rise of the Tea Party, support for the movement among the American public has remained steady. Polls show that somewhere between 10–20 percent of Americans consider themselves to be supporters of the Tea Party. However, it is clear that negative views of the Tea Party have risen sharply. In an October 2013 Pew Research Center poll, 49 percent of respondents had an unfavorable view of the Tea Party; this was nearly double the number from a 2010 poll. Many of those who had changed their view on the movement identified as moderate to liberal Republicans.

The Tea Party's role in government obstruction is debated in this chapter, which examines possible reasons for the gridlock and dysfunction impacting the federal government. Other viewpoints in the chapter consider the roles of partisan media and the lack of bipartisanship in the US Congress as part of the problem.

> "Divided government in Washington,
> more often than not, doesn't force par-
> ties to the center for compromise; it
> causes gridlock."

Divided Government Usually Means Gridlock

Emily Badger

Emily Badger is a writer. In the following viewpoint, she main-
tains that the purging of moderates from both political parties
has intensified political partisanship and divisions, leading to a
paralyzing gridlock and a US Congress unable to confront the
nation's challenges. Badger points out that in the past, Congress
has been able to pass important legislation despite party gridlock
because it had a large percentage of moderates who would work
together in a bipartisan manner. Today, she argues, that sense of
bipartisanship is missing, and the US Congress is populated with
ideological purists unwilling to compromise. In fact, she main-
tains, the majority of Republican candidates in the 2010 mid-
term elections campaigned on promises not to compromise with

Democrats in Congress. She predicts that the prospect of any significant legislation being passed by Congress under these conditions is low.

As you read, consider the following questions:

1. According to Professor Sarah Binder, what percentage of Congress members were political moderates in the 1960s and 1970s?

2. What does Binder consider to be the closest historical analogy to today's government gridlock?

3. What political movement does Badger identify as the one sending candidates to Congress with a no-compromise mandate?

Barack Obama stood behind the podium[1] at the White House on Wednesday after his party took a historic drubbing in the midterm elections and forecast the calm, constructive path that lies ahead. He will get together with Republican John Boehner,[2] the likely Speaker of the House come January, and Senate Minority Leader Mitch McConnell,[3] and together the long-warring politicians will find common ground on tax cuts, energy policy and job creation.

"What we're going to need to do, and what the American people want, is for us to mix and match ideas,[4] figure out those areas where we can agree on, move forward on those, and disagree without being disagreeable on those areas that we can't agree on," he said. "If we accomplish that, then there will be time for politics later."

This is a nice vision, and Obama's first White House social with the newly empowered Republicans has already been given a feel-good moniker: The Slurpee summit![5]

History, though, predicts a different scene. Sarah Binder,[6] a professor of political science at George Washington University and a senior fellow with the Brookings Institution, doubts

Obama and Boehner will agree on Slurpee flavors, much less any substantive policy in the two years to come. Divided government[7] in Washington, more often than not, doesn't force parties to the center for compromise; it causes gridlock.[8]

"The caveat is that we can't tell all that much from divided government alone," Binder said.

Divided government (also known by its nicer name, "shared power") has in the past produced some big things: the Clean Air Act[9] in the 1970s and tax reform[10] in the 1980s (both executed with Democratic Houses and Republican presidents), and welfare reform[11] in the 1990s (with a Democratic president and a Republican Congress). But those governments all had something the 112th Congress will lack in a big way.

"If you look back to the '60s and '70s, how could a divided government be so productive? Well, 30–40 percent of the chamber were ideological moderates," Binder said. "If you need large bipartisan majorities to get much done, and you don't have 60 votes by yourself, then moderates in the middle make a big difference. And we don't have any of that today."[12]

In fact, polarization in the Capitol—already at historic highs[13]—grew worse Tuesday night, with moderates heavily picked off by voters. The "Blue Dog" Democrats in the House lost half their caucus[14] on election night.

This means that we head into 2011 with a paralyzing pair of factors in Washington: Government is divided, and the two parties sit particularly far apart. There's no perfect historic analogy for this moment, Binder said, although the era ushered in by the 1994 midterms[15] may come closest.

"Things do get done in divided government," she warned. "But more gets left undone."

Even if the two parties are able to find areas where they can agree, as Obama suggests they can, that's not a promise of

" 'COLLEGIALITY' IS THE NEW WASHINGTON BUZZWORD. I HAD TO CHECK THE OXFORD ENGLISH DICTIONARY TO SEE EXACTLY WHAT IT MEANS."

© Harley Schwadron/CartoonStock.com.

compromise, either. Republicans, after all, found a pretty successful strategy the last two years in refusing to do just that, on principle.

Binder was stumped as to whether historic patterns can help predict when parties will behave this way—refusing to compromise as a political strategy in and of itself.

"For a while we all thought it had to do something with the size of the majority," she said. The smaller the in-party's majority, the more likely the minority party is to think control is within reach if it just digs in a little longer. "But [now] I'm not so sure about that. We've had oversized Democratic majorities and no less digging in of the heels by the Republican minority."

Some Republicans have been blunt about their intentions not to bend,[16] and the Tea Party is sending candidates to town explicitly with a no-compromise mandate. The best hope may be that the parties begrudgingly work together, each in search of the credit for reviving the economy.

But an energy bill, immigration reform, a deficit solution—history says they're not likely.

Links

1. http://www.whitehouse.gov/blog/2010/11/03/president-obama-s-press-conference-lets-find-those-areas-where-we-can-agree

2. http://www.nytimes.com/2010/11/03/us/politics/03boehner.html?_r=0

3. http://www.mcconnell.senate.gov/public/

4. http://blogs.suntimes.com/sweet/2010/11/obama_post-2010_election_press.html

5. http://www.whorunsgov.com/politerati/whos-news/nancypelosi-prepares-to-give-up-the-gavel-obama-likes-slurpee-summit-idea-whos-news-11-4/

6. http://home.gwu.edu/~binder/

7. http://uspolitics.about.com/od/usgovernment/l/bl_party_division_2.htm

8. http://www.brookings.edu/blogs/up-front/posts/2010/11/03-congress-binder

9. http://en.wikipedia.org/wiki/Clean_Air_Act

10. http://en.wikipedia.org/wiki/Tax_Reform_Act_of_1986

11. http://www.sourcewatch.org/index.php?title=1996_Personal_Responsibility_and_Work_Opportunity_Reconciliation_Act

12. http://www.psmag.com/navigation/politics-and-law/political-leapfrog-hops-over-most-americans-24883/

13. http://www.psmag.com/navigation/politics-and-law/there-is-no-common-ground-anymore-3412/

14. http://www.politico.com/blogs/glennthrush/1110/Blue_Dog_wipeout_Half_of_caucus_gone.html

15. http://en.wikipedia.org/wiki/Republican_Revolution

16. http://thehill.com/blogs/blog-briefing-room/news/125383-republicans-say-compromise-not-on-the-agenda

| "It is as if the incentive structure was engineered to promote gridlock."

Too Much Bipartisanship Is Responsible for Government Dysfunction

Andrew Levine

Andrew Levine is an author, a senior scholar at the Institute for Policy Studies, and a professor of philosophy at the University of Wisconsin–Madison. In the following viewpoint, he outlines the conventional wisdom on the state of American government: Democratic and Republican politicians are at one another's throats; Republican obstructionism has led to congressional gridlock, stifling both important legislation and key judicial and executive appointments; and government has ceased to function effectively. He argues that both Democrats and Republicans are eager to do the bidding of the wealthy and powerful and often work together to further enrich the wealthy at the expense of the rest of Americans. He is hopeful about an emerging coalition between libertarians and a number of Democrats concerned about protecting civil liberties, viewing it as one of the few encouraging signs on the horizon for American freedom.

As you read, consider the following questions:

1. According to Levine, what did Robert Frost say about liberals?

2. Who does Levine identify as the greatest whistleblower in American history?

3. According to Levine, by how many votes did an attempt to defund the NSA's phone data collection program fail on July 24, 2013?

The conventional wisdom on the state of the American government is disheartening. It is also convincing, as one would expect a hodgepodge of observations and common knowledge to be.

Common Knowledge

It is common knowledge, for example, that our government has become dysfunctional because Democrats and Republicans are at each other's throats.

Everybody knows what the remedy is: We need more bipartisanship. The government would become more functional if Democrats and Republicans cooperated more.

Everyone's well-being depends on a well-functioning government. Bipartisanship is therefore in everyone's interest.

On this, even the plutocrats are, or ought to be, on board. If anything, they need a functioning government more than the rest of us.

Too bad therefore that they sometimes find themselves so overcome by greed, and so blinded by the lure of short-term gains, that they do the wrong thing—not just for the country, but even for themselves.

This is one reason why we seem unable to get from here to there, from our current sorry state to a condition where government works at least as well as it did when Democrats and Republicans still got along tolerably well.

The problem has become worse now that the Supreme Court removed nearly all legal constraints on the ability of moneyed interests to game the system.

Its 2010 *Citizens United* ruling [referring to the Supreme Court decision in *Citizens United v. Federal Election Commission*] was not only disastrous for the ninety-nine percent. It also removed one of the ways that the one percent was saved from the consequences of its own rapaciousness and myopia.

Then, to make matters worse still, there are the characters who comprise the American political class.

In addition to their inherent limitations and lack of regard for the common good, electoral and pecuniary interests sometimes lead them to do all they can to placate constituents who will not tolerate compromises of any kind. This is especially true on the Republican side. Their "base" is sublimely obstinate.

In Democratic ranks, and in the White House, there are politicians aplenty who have taken Robert Frost's characterization of liberals to heart: They won't take their own side in an argument. They are so "reasonable" that they practically invite their more obdurate and mean-spirited colleagues to walk all over them.

The conventional wisdom therefore has it that bipartisanship is in short supply, that we would be better off if there were more of it, and that the obstacles in its way are daunting and perhaps insurmountable.

This is a plausible account of how things are; it explains a great deal.

But is it true? Are the assumptions underlying it correct? And are those who believe it looking at the situation the right way?

If we are to make things better, or at least to keep them from getting worse, coming to terms with these questions is of the utmost importance.

Bipartisanship

"Bipartisanship," neither the word nor the concept it expresses, plays no role in the great philosophical justifying theories of democratic institutions.

This is hardly surprising; those theories predate the rise of the party system in early nineteenth-century Europe and North America. It is telling, though, that no one has ever seen fit to update them by incorporating "bipartisanship" into their conceptual repertoire.

It is not just that the idea is of no inherent philosophical interest. It is more that it is a provincial concern. Even in a world where it has become normal for political parties to mediate between voters and the state, the American duopoly system is an outlier.

To be sure, what goes on in the empire's core is, almost by definition, not provincial. But this case is extreme enough to overcome the general rule.

In the United States, each state makes the rules that govern its electoral contests; the federal government's role is minimal and focused mainly on assuring that constitutional rights are respected.

And every state permits multiparty electoral competition. That, anyway, is the theory. In practice, they all make ballot access difficult, and they all do whatever they can to marginalize "third"—or fourth or fifth—parties. They are so effective that candidates who are not Democrats or Republicans have to struggle even to attract protest votes.

This is why when independents or third-party candidates gain electoral office, it is almost always at the local level; and it is often in "non-partisan" elections in which the party affiliations of the candidates aren't even known to most voters.

Then thanks to media disinterest, even the educational effects of political campaigns waged outside the prevailing duopoly structure are effectively nil.

I say this as someone who always votes, but almost never votes for Democrats; voting for Republicans is, of course, out of the question. But protest voting is cheap. If there were a way to distinguish abstention from indifference, not voting at all would be an even more fitting way to express a considered judgment.

The Role of Gridlock

But however that may be, for now and the foreseeable future, the fact that Democrats and Republicans dominate the political scene makes bipartisanship important—notwithstanding the fecklessness of Democrats and the malevolence of Republicans, and notwithstanding the irrelevance to democratic theory of how well or poorly they get along.

When bipartisanship is in short supply, as it now is, the system freezes up; there is gridlock. The more gridlock there is, the more the government is disabled.

This can be a good thing; it has so far prevented the [Barack] Obama administration from grand bargaining away the remaining gains of the New Deal–Great Society era. But, on balance, gridlock works to the detriment of us all.

This is an American phenomenon, but the reasons for it are institutional, not cultural. It would be the same anywhere that two semi-established parties monopolize the electoral scene.

Most observers nowadays, not just Democrats, take it for granted that Republicans are mainly to blame for bipartisanship's decline. They think that Republicans have either lost sight of its importance or else that they have chosen deliberately to disregard it.

If the latter, it may be because they or their constituents hate the president so much that they cannot bring themselves to cooperate even for the sake of the public good. There is truth in this; some anxious and benighted white folks do hate the president—for the wrong reasons.

Or perhaps Republicans think that a dysfunctional government will help bring them to power—and they care more about that than about the consequences of dysfunctional governance.

Whatever the reasons, from the moment Barack Obama assumed office, Republicans have done their level best to obstruct his every move.

Rarely have any of them said so directly, at least in circumstances where they might be overheard. But candor is scarce in Republican ranks; so too is self-understanding.

When Republican obstructionists do try to justify themselves, they gravitate towards one or another tenet of neoliberal ideology—"free market" theology—or they appeal to macroeconomic idiocies about the harmful effects of deficit spending and high levels of government debt in periods of slow or negative economic growth.

No doubt, many of them believe in the nostrums they propose, and their sincerity, if genuine, is estimable. But it hardly cancels out the harm their ill-conceived and mean-spirited policies cause.

It is noteworthy, however, that even in their most obstructionist moments, Republicans still uphold bipartisanship as an ideal. It is just that they want it on their terms—not their rival's.

And so, each side blames the other for keeping bipartisanship at bay.

The Search for the Holy Grail

Because Republican disingenuousness is palpable, and because Obama seems reasonable to a fault, he and his colleagues in the Democratic Party have the stronger case according to the common knowledge of most sensible people.

But this benefits him almost not at all when it comes to governance because, in our "democracy," it hardly matters what most people, much less reasonable people, think.

Nevertheless, for Obama especially, but not only for him, "bipartisanship" has become the Holy Grail. He seeks it relentlessly, and he is disappointed every time. Republican obduracy always gets in the way.

The remarkable thing is how maladroitly Obama pursues his quest. The more he tries and fails, the weaker—indeed, the more risible—he seems, and the less incentive Republicans have to go along. It is as if he wants to lose.

It could have been otherwise, and not just in the months after the 2008 election when Obama had political capital to spare. Were he and his fellow Democrats truly committed to "change," and were they less awful at strategizing or even just a little shrewder, they would have long ago figured out how they too could play the Republicans' game.

It is just a matter of leveraging their considerable, underutilized power by being less eager to give in.

Had they done so, they could have steered the legislative process in the directions they favor (or say they favor), just as the Tea Party has been doing from the moment it was concocted.

This may still be possible, though, at this point it is hard to see how anyone this side of the MSNBC evening lineup can still take Obama seriously.

But it isn't going to happen; Democrats are . . . constitutionally incapable of changing their ways, and Obama doesn't have it in him to govern effectively.

The future therefore promises more of the same; Republican obstinacy along with Democratic cluelessness and pusillanimity.

Were our capitalists more enlightened or were our parties less in lockstep ideologically, there might be a chance of breaking out of the circle. But, as things now are, there is no chance.

We have come to a point where radical solutions are necessary even for just restoring the business as usual of the still recent past.

To appreciate the depth of the problems afflicting us, we need to look beyond the obvious failings of Democrats, Republicans and capitalists blinded by greed.

We need to ask ourselves why, if they are all such blunder heads, they, the capitalists especially, are still prosperous and secure?

Perhaps the conventional wisdom has gotten it wrong. Perhaps the problem is not too little bipartisanship but too much.

Too Much Bipartisanship?

On matters that affect most of us, the ninety-nine percent, the conventional wisdom is plainly on track. Republicans, Democrats, and greedy, myopic capitalists have turned the American government into a dysfunctional laughingstock—to the detriment of one and all.

The perpetrators are not about to change their ways either. Even if they care about the consequences of what they have done, they don't care enough.

It is not that they are all mean-spirited though some surely are. It is that they don't see any percentage in turning the situation around.

This is especially true of the politicians; for them, following the money has become not just the main thing, but the only thing. The higher the office, the more money they need to be elected, and the more money there is for them when their days in government are through.

The need for dollars—millions, even billions of them— just to get into the game makes for a lethal confection, especially in conjunction with the structural pathologies of our not very democratic electoral system—its duopoly party structure, its first past the post elections, its gerrymandered electoral districts, and so on.

It is as if the incentive structure was engineered to promote gridlock. With so many disincentives to cooperate, it is a wonder that there is any bipartisanship at all.

The NSA Spying Scandal

In June [2013], newspaper articles revealed the existence of a vast, worldwide program of surveillance and electronic data collection by the U.S. National Security Agency (NSA). Documents leaked by a former NSA contractor, Edward Snowden, indicated that the Foreign Intelligence Surveillance Court, a judicial body whose proceedings are secret, had regularly authorized the NSA to capture records, or metadata, from the telephone and Internet communications of hundreds of millions of people in the United States and overseas. The statutory basis for this authorization came from Section 215 of the USA PATRIOT Act, enacted in the immediate aftermath of the 11 September 2001 terrorist attacks. Further disclosures revealed that U.S. intelligence agencies had tapped the phones of dozens of foreign leaders, including German chancellor Angela Merkel, who forcefully protested the monitoring of her mobile phone....

On 17 January 2014, Obama gave a speech on the NSA spying controversy. He declared that surveillance of allied foreign governments would cease and that he was opposed to the NSA keeping a database of communication records, suggesting that the data storage be taken out of government hands. While acknowledging civil liberties concerns, Obama defended the central components of NSA intelligence gathering as essential for protecting national security against terrorist threats.

"Espionage,"
Global Issues in Context Online Collection.
Detroit, MI: Gale, 2014.

Add in the animosity Obama elicits in the darkest corners of our far from post-racist society, and it is a perfect storm.

The old slogan "the only solution, revolution" has seemed quaintly anachronistic for decades, and at no time more so, at least in the United States, than in the Age of Obama.

But the time is past due to rethink all that. Now that increasing numbers of people are beginning to see through the miasma that is Obama's medium and message, the prospects for doing so are at last beginning to improve. . . .

On matters that affect the fraction of the one percent that the Obama administration exists to serve, the conventional wisdom is at least partly on track as well.

There is, after all, a bipartisan consensus on ends; both parties want to do what is best for their paymasters. However, when it comes to deciding on means, the consensus breaks down—in part.

Capitalist myopia and greed, along with conflicting economic doctrines, driven partly by ideological biases and partly by honest disagreements, leave Democrats and Republicans frequently at odds, among themselves and with each other.

But when there are clear and unequivocal class interests at stake, there is bipartisanship aplenty.

Cooperation When It Counts

This is why bankers have had carte blanche to loot the economy, why corporations, not people or even major cities like Detroit, get bailed out when they fall into dire financial straits, why everything necessary to keep stock prices high gets done, and why, in general, corporate interests take precedence over peoples' interests.

When economic elites are of one mind, Democrats and Republicans are in accord, and there is all the bipartisanship anyone could want.

The ruling class is sufficiently united, too, to keep the functionaries who run our ever-expanding military–national security state complex from breaking free of its grasp by constituting an independent power source of their own.

But this does not keep the generals and spymasters from calling the shots in Congress and the White House. In matters of concern to them, there is bipartisanship to spare.

The Obama administration's war on the conditions for democratic governance—above all, its efforts to assure that Americans be uninformed—is of preeminent concern to the military–security state complex. Needless to say, it has broad bipartisan support.

Hence the unflinching backing the leaderships of both parties—and their media flunkies—accord to Obama and his attorney general, Eric Holder, as they go after Edward Snowden, arguably the greatest whistleblower in American history.

Snowden is guilty only of embarrassing our "yes, we scan" president, Hillary Clinton's State Department, and of course the Pentagon, the CIA [Central Intelligence Agency], the NSA [National Security Agency] and the countless other government agencies that make a mockery of the idea of the rule of law.

A government under law that abides by the spirit of the laws was what the authors of our Constitution proclaimed, even as they supported or permitted slavery and the extermination of the indigenous peoples of North America.

Despite their hypocrisies and inconsistencies, their vision inspired the experiment in government of, by and for the people that Abraham Lincoln would later exalt.

That experiment has never been easy. Just with respect to slavery and its consequences, it took a Civil War and a hundred years of struggle for anything like political, equality or equal justice under law to be approximated.

In time, however, the vision of our republic's founders was more or less realized.

Now, though, on the transparently fatuous pretext of fighting terrorism, our bipartisan rulers want to turn back these basic liberal and democratic achievements.

Snowden's revelations threaten their ambitions, and that they cannot abide.

This is also what explains their assault on WikiLeaks and its leader, Julian Assange, and the shameful show trial of Bradley Manning.

It has gotten so bad that there is no longer any point even in remarking sarcastically on how the University of Chicago once entrusted Obama to teach constitutional law. That would be almost as pointless as going on about the drone president's Nobel Prize for peace.

The man has done his best to undo the constitutional protections that were our glory even in imperialism's vilest moments.

As the Vietnam War raged, we Americans could at least take solace in the fact that the First, Fifth and especially the Fourth Amendments protected us; that we could count on free speech, due process and freedom from "unreasonable" searches and seizures.

Today instead we have a bipartisan consensus that none of that really matters. It is hard to believe, but it is happening nevertheless.

Who Will Challenge the Power Structure?

Rare are the Democrats who will challenge the president on this account, except in the mildest of ways. There is ample evidence from polling data that the American people are appalled by the extent of government surveillance. But, within the political class, there is only scant resistance and most of it comes from the libertarian fringes of the GOP.

Nevertheless, a vote last week [July 24, 2013] to defund the NSA's phone data collection program failed by only eleven votes. But for intense White House lobbying and the combined efforts of the leaderships of both parties, it would almost certainly have passed.

Is this a harbinger of a new bipartisanship, a union of anti-Obama Republicans and backbench Democrats fed up with the administration's lackadaisical attitude toward civil liberties?

It is not impossible; there are certainly plenty of voters ready to say "enough!" to Big Brother and his wars, and not all of them usually vote for Democrats.

But don't count on it. When push comes to shove, Democrats will rally around their commander in chief, no matter how unpopular his policies may be, and they will lack the courage to stand up to their party's leadership. As for Republicans, even if a few of them genuinely do have a libertarian streak, the vast majority of them remain as idiotic and obstinate as ever.

However, the vote on defunding the NSA may well be an indicator of something else—of how there are people, many of them, outside the constituencies that traditionally vote Democratic, who can be won over to fighting the real enemy—the fraction of the one percent that owns both political parties and for whom the government and its overblown military and security services work.

That might just be a basis for the radical solutions required genuinely to restore functional governance, and it might also be instrumental for saving what remains of the social and economic progress achieved in the New Deal–Great Society era. It could even be a basis for moving forward again.

Such a development would have very little to do with bipartisanship, bottom up or otherwise. But it could have a great deal to do with bringing democracy to the USA.

> *"Gridlock, partisan polarisation, and the rightward thrust in contemporary American politics derive from the Tea Party's takeover of the Republican Party, which in turn has enabled the Tea Party to paralyse Congress and the entire American government."*

The Tea Party Is Escalating Political Gridlock

Mark Kesselman

Mark Kesselman is professor emeritus of political science at Columbia University and senior editor of International Political Science Review. *In the following viewpoint, he identifies the Tea Party as the source of the current gridlock in Washington, arguing that before the emergence of the Tea Party, there was still a tradition of compromise, despite party division in government. Kesselman suggests that Tea Party supporters are motivated, well funded by outside interests, and well organized. These factors enabled them to move Republican politicians to the far right, despite the fact that the movement does not have widespread sup-*

port among American voters. Kesselman concludes that as the Republican Party becomes more radicalized and extreme, congressional gridlock will become a regular feature of US governance.

As you read, consider the following questions:

1. According to the author, how many federal employees were nearly furloughed in April 2011 when Congress could not agree to raise the debt ceiling?

2. According to the viewpoint, in what year did the Tea Party movement emerge?

3. What controversial billionaire brothers give lavish financial support to the Tea Party, according to Kesselman?

For generations, American political leaders have proclaimed the exceptional virtues of the country's political system. Official agencies, including the State Department, United States Agency for International Development (USAID), and National Endowment for Democracy, provide assistance for American-style democracy promotion to governments around the world. So do the International Republican Institute and National Democratic Institute for International Affairs— government-funded organisations affiliated with the major American political parties. However, the near failure to avert the so-called "fiscal cliff" in late December [2012], coming on the heels of other recent spectacles of government dysfunction, prompts the question: Why should the American political system serve as a model for other countries to emulate?

The American Taxpayer Relief Act of 2012, passed at the 11th hour (in fact, it was passed after the official deadline of December 31, 2012—near midnight on January 1, 2013), is a short-term fix to the self-imposed fiscal crisis. The last-minute agreement simply postponed the day(s) of reckoning for several months. Nor was the recent cliffhanger unprecedented. For years, American political institutions have apparently been in a state of near-paralysis (the qualifier—"apparently"—is intended to convey the fact that the system is working just fine for the top few percent, who for the past several decades have appropriated most of the benefits generated by economic growth). For example, in April 2011 the government was nearly forced to shut down all nonessential federal services and furlough 800,000 federal employees because Congress refused to pass a budget. Later that year, on August 2, 2011, with the US only hours away from reaching the deadline to avoid defaulting on the federal debt, Congress voted to raise the debt ceiling.

It was this pattern that prompted two political analysts to publish a scathing critique of congressional dysfunctions in early 2012 with the disturbing title *It's Even Worse than It Looks*. In a recent article updating their account, they went further: "[We] thought that the 112th Congress was the worst we had seen in our four decades in Washington. However, [recent events] . . . convinced us that it was the worst Congress ever." What explains the current gridlock in Washington?

Gridlock

Passage of the American Taxpayer Relief Act of 2012 enabled Congress to prevent falling off the so-called fiscal cliff—shorthand for legislation that, but for passage of the Taxpayer Relief Act, mandated increases in income taxes for all Americans and steep cuts in military and civilian spending. Instead, the Taxpayer Relief Act raises taxes for the small number of Americans whose annual taxable income exceeds $400,000 and left income tax rates unchanged for other Americans. However, because the agreement did not extend a previously enacted cut in the payroll tax, levied to finance social programmes, the net income of all working Americans and their families has been reduced. The agreement postponed for two months the substantial reduction in military and civilian programmes that had been scheduled to begin January 1, 2013. In effect, the agreement invited Congress to address the issue of spending cuts before the impending March deadline.

While the agreement forestalled major fiscal disruption for the time being, it was a ramshackle and inadequate attempt to deal with the problems that it was ostensibly designed to solve. The culmination of a protracted, tragi-comic, and embarrassing spectacle, the American Taxpayer Relief Act of 2012 (to paraphrase Winston Churchill) was not the end, nor even the beginning of the end. In less than two months, we may learn that it was not even the end of the beginning.

A place to begin to explain Washington's current dysfunctional condition is the basic design of American political institutions, notably, the presidential system that allocates the executive and legislature independent powers. In contrast to a parliamentary system of fused powers, the separation of powers creates a built-in, that is, structural, potential for gridlock when each branch is controlled by an opposing party. The Constitution specifies that, in order for legislation to be adopted, a bill must be voted on by both houses of Congress and approved by the president. This requirement invites deadlock when opposing parties control different political institutions. Moreover, congressional procedures further constrain reform. For example, the Senate's current filibuster rule specifies that a supermajority—60 of the 100-member body—must support bringing a measure to the floor for a vote. In the House, the Speaker (that is, the leader of the majority party in the chamber) can prevent proposals from being scheduled for a vote. During the recent imbroglio over the fiscal cliff, House Republican Speaker John A. Boehner refused to allow the House to vote on a measure passed by the Senate and supported by the president.

Granted that the present political conjuncture, in which the Democratic Party controls the presidency and Senate, and the Republican Party the House of Representatives, creates the possibility for gridlock. However, the separation of powers, even with divided partisan control, does not *guarantee* gridlock. During previous periods in American history, divided government did not prevent compromise. In the 1980s, Republican president Ronald Reagan and Democratic Speaker of the House Thomas ("Tip") O'Neill Jr. famously delivered bombastic partisan speeches during the day—after which they adjourned to the White House family quarters to socialise. Their camaraderie enabled them to negotiate political compromises across the partisan and ideological divide.

Reagan's and O'Neill's example has prompted some analysts to attribute the current gridlock to flaws in the personalities and governing styles of incumbent political leaders. Speaker Boehner has been criticised for lacking charisma and an ability to garner support from his Republican colleagues for deals that he has negotiated.

Political Polarisation?

President Obama's performance has come under especially close scrutiny. He has been faulted for maintaining an arms-length relationship with members of Congress. If only, so goes the critique, he invited them for a round of golf or dinner at the White House, opponents might be induced to become partners. Obama was also criticised for "out-sourcing" the recent fiscal negotiations to Vice President Joseph Biden. Political analyst Jonathan Chait has characterised Obama's negotiating style by a dismissive term from poker: "Tight-weak . . . the worst of all worlds—when you have a weak hand, you lose, and when you have a strong hand you fail to maximise your position." Chait claims that during the fiscal negotiations, Obama needlessly squandered the gains he had amassed from his reelection.

The personalities of key players may partially explain why gridlock occurs. However, some highly successful political leaders in the past were hardly great negotiators. Moreover, Barack Obama has exquisite oratorical ability and John Boehner has demonstrated the ability to obtain sufficient support from his troops for choices they found highly distasteful. It is not persuasive to reduce Washington's current dysfunction to the failings of political leaders.

Until recently, material incentives, known as earmarks, helped soften the hard edges of ideology and induced legislators to reach deals across the partisan divide. Earmarks, also known as pork barrel spending, involve expenditures authorised by Congress that are designated for specific local public works projects—a grant to build a public hospital in an Indiana county, a road in rural Nebraska, the famous "bridge to nowhere" in Alaska (that figured in the 2008 presidential campaign). Incumbent legislators reap electoral rewards from earmarks by bringing home the bacon for their constituents. Congress prohibited earmarks several years ago, in response to pressure from the antigovernment, antispending movement known as the Tea Party (more about the Tea Party below). This reform has significantly reduced the incentive for legislators to reach bipartisan compromises.

Many observers attribute gridlock to partisan polarisation, that is, deep divisions between the Democratic and Republican parties in which compromise is considered to be a liability rather than a virtue. It is indisputable that the two parties are far apart on issues and unwilling to compromise. But describing the problem as partisan polarisation implies that the two parties are equally far from the centre of the political continuum, as measured by the policy preferences of their respective electorates or leaders and by the substance of their policy positions.

Tea Time

In fact, polarisation is not symmetrical: The Republican Party (GOP) is much further to the right than the Democratic Party is to the left; and it is far less willing to compromise. Therefore, explaining gridlock requires understanding what has produced the Republican Party's rightward ideological shift and intransigence. The answer can be provided in one—or rather, three—words: The Tea Party! Gridlock, partisan polarisation, and the rightward thrust in contemporary American politics derive from the Tea Party's takeover of the Republican Party, which in turn has enabled the Tea Party to paralyse Congress and the entire American government.

The Tea Party movement erupted in 2009, soon after the election of the first African American president in American history, a Democrat who was markedly more liberal than his Republican predecessor. The Tea Party is an ideological outlier within American politics, given its fierce opposition to tax increases; strong support for a minimal federal government achieved by substantial cuts in federal spending on social programmes (or, preferably, their privatisation); and harsh immigration policies. The Tea Party's refusal to bargain and compromise also contrasts with what has often been described as typical American pragmatism.

Their influence is disproportionate to the number of its supporters or elected officials. Its major source of power is the Republican-controlled House of Representatives. *New York Times* columnist Ross Douthat has observed that because the Republican Party controls the House of Representatives, it "has much more power in Washington than it has support in the nation as a whole". While only about one-quarter of House Republicans belong to the Tea Party congressional caucus, the Tea Party's ideological influence in the House Republican caucus, coupled with Republican control of the House of Representatives, have gridlocked the American political system since 2010.

The Tea Party's direct influence can be measured by the number of Republican officials in Congress and at state and local levels who owe their election to its support. However, the movement's indirect influence within the Republican Party reaches far beyond its officeholders. The Tea Party has reshaped the orientation of the entire Republican Party toward the hard-edged right; it has been remarkably successful in intimidating Republican officeholders, including those who may not share its extreme positions. What explains these remarkable achievements?

Their major weapon is the movement's ability to influence Republican primaries: Tea Party–backed candidates have often been able to defeat more popular and less extreme incumbent officeholders and aspirants for Republican nominations. What explains the Tea Party's success?

The Tea Party's outsized influence primarily derives from the fact that its supporters are well organised whereas rank-and-file Republicans are relatively dispersed. The fact that Tea Party supporters vote in high proportions in Republican primaries enables them to nominate candidates whose positions are at odds with those of rank-and-file Republicans. Similarly, Republican officeholders may support Tea Party positions less from genuine conviction than from fear of having to face off against a Tea Party–backed candidate at the next primary (the Tea Party also benefits from the lavish financial support of affluent ultraconservatives, including the billionaire brothers Charles and David Koch).

A good example of Tea Party influence occurred during the negotiations last December to devise a compromise to forestall the fiscal cliff. Speaker Boehner designed what he dubbed Plan B as a Republican alternative to the Democratic proposal to raise income taxes for Americans with annual incomes over $250,000. Plan B included a threshold for a tax increase for those with $1 million in annual income. Thus, the projected increase would affect only the richest 0.2 percent of Americans. Passage of Plan B by the Republican-controlled House of Representatives would have been purely symbolic since it would surely have been defeated by the Democratic-controlled Senate. Boehner introduced Plan B to signal Republicans' willingness to negotiate. However, shortly before the House was scheduled to vote, Boehner withdrew the measure. The reason was that, because of a revolt by Tea Party sympathizers—who opposed raising taxes for even the wealthiest Americans—Boehner was forced to announce that Plan B lacked sufficient Republican support to ensure passage. The debacle opened the way for a compromise plan negotiated by Vice President Joseph Biden and Mitch McConnell, Senate minority leader (a Republican). The measure was overwhelmingly approved by the Senate and approved in the House by most Democrats and several dozen Republicans (including Boehner). Passage of the American Taxpayer Relief Act of 2012 briefly ended the threat of the fiscal cliff—albeit not with a bang but a whimper.

Pushed to the Right

The American Taxpayer Relief Act of 2012, passed barely in time to snatch victory from the jaws of defeat, provides meager cause for rejoicing. At best, it briefly postponed dealing with America's fiscal and economic problems. The imminent arrival of three deadlines in the next two months will inevitably generate additional titanic battles.

First, by late February Congress must approve an increase in the $16.4 trillion debt limit. Failure to do so will produce a US default on the government's debt and would jeopardise the financial stability of the US and possibly the entire global economy. Nonetheless, numerous Republican senators have signalled that they plan to use the possibility of default as a bargaining chip, i.e., that their support for an increase in the debt limit depends on whether Congress mandates additional spending cuts.

Second, the American Taxpayer Relief Act postponed for two months previously mandated budget sequestrations involving substantial automatic spending cuts, split equally between military and civilian programmes. Unless Congress

Fifteen Core Beliefs of the Tea Party

1. Illegal aliens are here illegally.

2. Pro-domestic employment is indispensable.

3. A strong military is essential.

4. Special interests must be eliminated.

5. Gun ownership is sacred.

6. Government must be downsized.

7. The national budget must be balanced.

8. Deficit spending must end.

9. Bailout and stimulus plans are illegal.

10. Reducing personal income taxes is a must.

11. Reducing business income taxes is mandatory.

12. Political offices must be available to average citizens.

13. Intrusive government must be stopped.

14. English as our core language is required.

15. Traditional family values are encouraged.

"15 Non-negotiable Core Beliefs,"
Teaparty.org, 2014.

agrees to reduce the federal budget deficit by a comparable amount, the cuts are scheduled to begin in early March.

Third, in late March, the federal government will have exhausted the funds that have been appropriated for its activities. Unless Congress appropriates additional funds, the government will be required to shut down nonessential services.

If any of these disruptions were to occur, the result would be highly destructive. Whether they will be avoided depends largely on the outcome of a current battle within the Republican Party. Broadly speaking, it pits supporters of the Tea Party against those who advocate modifying the party's ideological extremism and intransigence in order to avoid continued electoral defeat and fiscal calamity.

Republican losses in 2012 have generated some pushback against the right-wing ultras. For example, in an implicit *mea culpa*, Ralph Reed, founder of the ultraconservative Faith and Freedom Coalition and former leader of the Christian Coalition, recently warned, "The Republican Party can't stay exactly where it is and stick its head in the sand...."

However, due to Tea Party pressure, there remains strong resistance to change within the Republican Party. After a majority of House Republicans voted to support the recent fiscal agreement, including the tax increase for Americans with incomes over $400,000, the *New York Times* observed "...[A]cross the country, deeply conservative organisations angry about the concession on tax increases are pledging more, not fewer, primary challenges to Republicans they believe are straying too far from the party's orthodoxy...." For example, the founder of the Florida Tea Party movement warned Republicans: "The gloves are off. We're going to challenge a lot of the GOP going forward."

Institutional Factors

Since the GOP's electoral setbacks have demonstrated that its extremist stance is unpopular with the electorate, what prevents the party from moderating its positions? For an answer, recall the institutional factors reviewed above. By and large, the "ultras" represent safe Republican districts—made even safer by redistricting when, following the 2010 midterm elections, the high point of Tea Party influence, Republican-controlled state legislatures redrew district lines to favour Republicans. The result has not only damaged Democratic prospects: Republican incumbents in safe Republican districts who stray from hard-right orthodoxy risk a 2014 primary challenge on their right.

What might overcome this logjam in the Republican Party? If the ultras continue to block change and are blamed for the resulting gridlock, the Republican Party might lose control of the House of Representatives in the 2014 midterm elections despite the advantage redistricting has provided. Consequently, the Democratic Party would preside over unified government and, for the time being, gridlock would end.

However, crystal-ball gazing is rarely fruitful. A preferable way to conclude would be to repeat the opening suggestion: Rather than extolling the excellence of their democracy, American political leaders might better devote attention to strengthening the quality of American democracy.

> "The Tea Party appears to have lost much of the media presence, grassroots energy, organizational backbone, and fund-raising clout that powered it in 2010."

The Tea Party Influence on American Politics Is Waning

Molly Ball

Molly Ball is a journalist and staff writer for the Atlantic. *In the following viewpoint, she observes that Democrats and establishment Republicans will not be able to scapegoat the Tea Party for government gridlock and political polarization for much longer because the movement's influence has been waning. Ball attributes this trend to decreasing media support, especially from Fox News; a growing wariness from establishment Republicans, who are frustrated with the movement's demands; a loss of grassroots energy and fund-raising clout; and an inconsistent record in electing Tea Party candidates to public office. The test of the Tea Party's clout will be in future primary elections, but establishment Republicans will be well served to focus on electing quality candidates who can stand up to Tea Party opposition, Ball asserts.*

As you read, consider the following questions:

1. Who does political commentator Dave Weigel identify as the Tea Party's preferred 2016 presidential candidate?

2. According to Ball, how many Republicans voted for the 2013 budget deal?

3. What Tea Party candidate lost in his attempt to become governor of Virginia in 2012?

The Tea Party has become a convenient scapegoat for both the left and the establishment right. If it weren't for these nasty reactionaries, both groups fret, Washington would not be gridlocked, Republicans (nice, sane ones) would be able to win some elections outside the most rock-ribbed, gerrymandered districts, and our political climate would not be beset by so much nastiness and vitriol. Contemplating the imminent defeat of Barry Goldwater in the fall 1964 issue of *Partisan Review*, Richard Schlatter of Rutgers University (quoted in Rick Perlstein's *Before the Storm*) wrote that it had "demonstrated that we are all part of the American Establishment." Today's Tea Party has created a similar sense of solidarity, as the writers of the "Is the Party Over?" symposium show.

Theda Skocpol argues that the Tea Party continues to have a powerful hold on the Republican Party, and that "this radical movement" isn't going anywhere, despite pundits' repeated, optimistic reports of its demise. Alan Abramowitz posits that the movement has badly damaged the Republican Party and cowed GOP leaders into submitting to its unpopular goals. Sean Wilentz insists that the antigovernment zeal of the Tea Partiers shouldn't be compared to Jacksonian [referring to the political ideas of President Andrew Jackson] populism, which defended the Union against both rogue states and moneyed interests. Leslie H. Gelb and Michael Kramer point to the GOP's ongoing confusion when it comes to foreign policy, with the Tea Party driving a strain of "hawkish isolationism" reminiscent of Goldwater. Christopher S. Parker says Tea Partiers' opposition to [Barack] Obama isn't "driven solely by racial resentment," but by "a more general perception of social change"; somewhat perplexingly, he then confidently predicts that the movement will lose intensity once Obama is out of office and "go underground" altogether if a white male Democrat becomes president. And Dave Weigel notes that Tea Partiers will be better prepared for the 2016 nomination battle and already appear to have a strong potential champion in Texas senator Ted Cruz. With the possible exception of Parker, whose argument contradicts itself, all seem to darkly foresee, in the words of Gelb and Kramer, "a stronger, even more vociferous Tea Party," with pernicious effects on the American polity.

Democrats like to blame the Tea Party for everything because it satisfies their conviction that the GOP is captive to extreme interests; the Republican establishment does so because it allows elites to evade blame for the party's electoral and philosophical failures. I don't want to be the latest in the long line of writers to pronounce the Tea Party on its deathbed, only to have it flare up and prove me wrong. As Skocpol rightly notes, the Tea Party's widely distributed, passionately engaged grassroots network combines with the clout of well-funded advocacy groups to create a potent squeeze on lawmakers from above and below. Last summer's fight over defunding Obamacare [referring to the Patient Protection and Affordable Care Act], and the government shutdown that resulted, showed that, if anything, the movement's activists have only become more aggressive in wielding this power. Incumbent Republican senators, even quite conservative ones like Mitch McConnell and John Cornyn, face primary challengers who see them as excessively conciliatory; House Speaker John Boehner seems helplessly in thrall to his caucus's most radical members and the outside agitators that egg them on. (Or he did—more on that in a bit.) Cruz clearly isn't going anywhere, and the next election could well deliver him still more allies in his Washington-based war on Washington.

The Fall of the Tea Party

Nonetheless, in relative terms, I see a Tea Party whose influence is gradually declining, not increasing. Its clout in Congress appears to be on the wane. Its ability to win intra-GOP contests is being newly challenged. And the organizational advantages it once enjoyed are no longer so clear-cut. The GOP rank and file that greeted the movement as an exciting infusion of new energy now regard it with weariness and skepticism. The far right, in turn, has focused much of its ire on the Republican Party itself, with increasing threats to start a third-party splinter movement. This seems unlikely to happen, but it reflects Tea Partiers' frustration at their inability to control the GOP more fully.

We should not, however, expect a waning Tea Party to mean a suddenly rosy political landscape. The [George W.] Bush years weren't exactly the glory days of bipartisan compromise, and the parties' major philosophical differences remain. Well before the Tea Party proved its clout in 2010, Obamacare failed to get a single Republican vote, and cap and trade was hung out to dry. And while anguished GOP elites love to wring their hands about how to bring to heel the crazies in their midst, there's little evidence they're any better at winning modern elections than the insurgents they disdain.

A Very Different Landscape

I have the advantage of writing this just after December's bipartisan budget deal [in 2013], the first time Congress has passed a full budget (as opposed to a continuing resolution) since 2009 and a promising signal for bipartisan compromise. The political and legislative landscape now looks very different from the immediate aftermath of the government shutdown, on which many of the symposium's writers based their conclusions. (In time, this apparent thaw may appear just as temporary and oversold as the shutdown's effects do now—although it does mean no one, not even Cruz, can shut down the government until at least October, when the current appropriations bills run out.)

It now appears that the Tea Party and its allied infrastructure—the Tea Party Industrial Complex—are no longer in charge of Boehner and the House GOP. Groups like Heritage Action [for America], the Senate Conservatives Fund, and the Club for Growth confronted a politician in Paul Ryan, the broker of the budget deal, who had enough credibility that he couldn't be shouted down with cries of "RINO!" Their cheerleading for the pointless defund-Obamacare strategy lost them the trust of the vast middle swath of House GOPers who consider themselves conservative but not irresponsible. Cruz has seen his stock fall with his Senate colleagues, several of whom excoriated him at a private lunch during the shutdown. And the Texan seems to have been at least slightly cowed: Though he took a position against the budget deal, he didn't stage a filibuster or otherwise crusade against it.

In the end, 169 Republicans—nearly three-quarters of the caucus—voted for the deal, flouting threats from the outside groups, whom Boehner took the opportunity to berate. (The normally stoic Speaker famously clutched the sides of his podium and cried, "Are you kidding me?" when asked about the conservative groups denouncing the deal.) Now, aides to House Republicans tell me there's a sense of relief that Boehner has finally seized the tiller. The House GOP remains extremely conservative and isn't going to suddenly start passing a bunch of liberal legislation. But there's a feeling that the chaotic caucus may now be less whipsawed by outside forces.

Future Challenges

The next test will be the upcoming round of GOP primaries. Skocpol speculates that "when it comes to 'reining in' the Tea

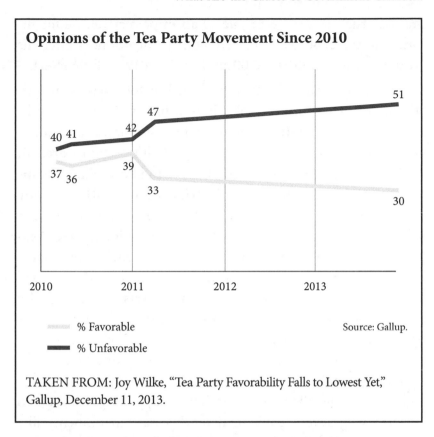

Opinions of the Tea Party Movement Since 2010

51

47

42

40 41

37 36

39

33

30

2010   2011   2012   2013

.... % Favorable   Source: Gallup.

▬▬ % Unfavorable

TAKEN FROM: Joy Wilke, "Tea Party Favorability Falls to Lowest Yet," Gallup, December 11, 2013.

Party, business associations and spokespeople may talk bigger than they will act." Perhaps. They've certainly failed to contain it in the past. Some of their tactics have been shockingly clumsy: The base reacted rather badly when the *New York Times* last year reported on the creation of the Conservative Victory Project, a primary-intervention initiative funded by the Karl Rove–led American Crossroads PAC [political action committee]. The front-page story framed the project as an effort to stop Iowa congressman Steve King from becoming a senator. (King has since decided to remain in the House.) In an antiestablishment political climate, there's an inherent difficulty in the establishment's efforts to reassert itself: Its support can easily be turned against the candidates it favors, as their opponents pillory them for being in cahoots with the forces of the old order. Rove, meanwhile, is an imperfect vehicle for reform, having reportedly lost credibility with donors after his groups spent more than $300 million in 2012 to little effect.

The Conservative Victory Project, I'm told, has been quietly mothballed. But the establishment hasn't given up on taking back the party. If anything, it has redoubled its efforts, and it is too soon to declare them a failure. Unprepared in 2010, snakebit and in denial in 2012, Republican elites are approaching this task with a new seriousness in 2014. Already there have been some modest successes. The November 2013 off-off-year elections were hailed as a victory for the GOP establishment: In a deep-red Alabama House district, the Chamber of Commerce–backed candidate won a GOP primary against a rabble-rousing birther; Chris Christie, the establishment's once-and-perhaps-future darling, trounced his opponent in New Jersey, while Tea Party favorite Ken Cuccinelli lost in Virginia, a GOP defeat that nonetheless bolstered the establishment's argument for what constitutes electability. Now, the chamber and other groups are gearing up to take sides as never before to defend Senate incumbents like McConnell, Thad Cochran, and Pat Roberts, and campaign for their favored candidates in open primaries.

Lost Advantages

The Tea Party had a number of advantages in 2010 that it doesn't have today. First and foremost, it had the element of surprise. Its sudden rise shocked the establishment and the public, seeming to come from nowhere to put fringe candidates on the map. Second, it had a powerful media megaphone in Fox News, which hyped the initial 2009 protests, especially on the show of then host Glenn Beck, who became the movement's unofficial leader and drew tens of thousands of followers to rallies. Today, Fox appears to have loosened that enthusiastic embrace (to the point that some conservatives now complain that Fox has gone soft), and Beck no longer has his platform at the channel.

Finally, the 2010 Tea Party threw major resources into the fights in which it intervened, deftly mastering grassroots fund-raising so that a candidate like Sharron Angle was able, staggeringly, to out-fund-raise the Senate majority leader. Today, many of the organizations that harnessed that energy are in disarray: FreedomWorks is wobbling after the messy ouster of front man Dick Armey, the former House majority leader, who took an $8 million buyout. The founders of the Tea Party Patriots have also split. The Tea Party Express, which buoyed candidates with a Sarah Palin–headlined bus tour in 2010, retains its association with the former vice-presidential nominee, but it seems safe to say a Palin-powered bus tour wouldn't generate the hype it once did. The groups newly taking up the Tea Party mantle have more diverse goals and motives, and the new class of challengers isn't thriving financially. McConnell raised $2.3 million between July and September 2013, while his primary challenger, Matt Bevin, raised just $800,000—$600,000 of it Bevin's own money.

The Tea Party appears to have lost much of the media presence, grassroots energy, organizational backbone, and fund-raising clout that powered it in 2010. That's not to say it couldn't have an impact in select races, and doesn't still have vocal proponents in Congress. But where it was once the engine of the GOP base, it is now more properly regarded as one faction among many in the Republican coalition—and a poorly organized, arriviste faction at that. Social conservatives, by comparison, have been organizing within the GOP for years, creating important, lasting grassroots power centers. That's why Rick Santorum was able to rise at the last moment and become the alternative to [Mitt] Romney in the 2012 primaries: Once social conservatives in Iowa and elsewhere finally settled on him as their choice, they were able to mobilize for him quickly and effectively. The Tea Party has not demonstrated a similar ability to unify and get out the vote.

Lingering Questions

The real question is whether the establishment's favored candidates will actually do any better than the Tea Partiers the GOP grandees are taking such pains to stop. It's true that far-right candidates Richard Mourdock in Indiana and Todd Akin in Missouri threw away 2012 Senate races that would have otherwise been winnable for the GOP. But establishment favorites in other states—many of whom made it through crowded primaries by touting their electability—didn't exactly prove that there's public hunger for moderate, pro-business conservatives. Connie Mack in Florida, Pete Hoekstra in Michigan, Denny Rehberg in Montana, Heather Wilson in New Mexico, Rick Berg in North Dakota, George Allen in Virginia, Tommy Thompson in Wisconsin: All were well-credentialed, establishment-anointed traditional candidates, and all lost their races in winnable states. In Massachusetts, Scott Brown's centrist appeal was no match for a crusading liberal, Elizabeth Warren, who was regarded as extreme by some in her own party. And then, of course, there's Mitt Romney, the very model of a pragmatic, economics-focused, business-class Republican, whom Democrats nonetheless depicted as out of touch with women, minorities, and the working class.

The establishment has spent much of the last few years blaming the Tea Party for the GOP's failures to win the Senate and the presidency. The Tea Party's response? "Physician, heal thyself."

> *"The growing personalization of media sources has yielded a world of competing commentators who, with few exceptions, stake out the rigid edge of their piece of the political spectrum."*

The Role of Partisan Media

Michael Kranish

Michael Kranish is an author, journalist, and deputy chief of the Boston Globe's Washington division. In the following viewpoint, he maintains that the proliferation of partisan media outlets in the 1980s and 1990s has resulted in historic levels of political polarization. Kranish suggests that these extreme voices on both sides of the political spectrum have often drowned out more moderate voices and have influenced the national debate. In many cases, partisan media personalities have created an echo chamber, where extreme ideas are discussed openly and considered mainstream. Kranish explains that a number of conservative media personalities in the genre have built media empires and wield influence in conservative circles and the Republican

Party. He says that critics of partisan media worry about the toxic effect these media outlets and personalities are having on national politics.

As you read, consider the following questions:

1. According to Kranish, how many signatures did Senator Ted Cruz get to defund Obamacare after appearing on Sean Hannity's Fox News television program?

2. How many talk radio stations were there in 2007, according to the viewpoint?

3. According to the viewpoint, how many Americans watch the three evening network news broadcasts today?

The host on Fox News Channel was chipper as ever one morning earlier this year [2013] as he welcomed the network's newest commentator, former US representative Allen West. The Florida Republican was on to discuss his astonishing claim: US Attorney General Eric Holder was a "bigger threat to our Republic" than the leader of al-Qaeda and was guilty of "treason from within."

It was ideological napalm, and *Fox & Friends* was happy to play along. The producer put up images of Holder and Osama bin Laden's successor, Ayman al-Zawahiri. Fox host Brian Kilmeade sounded pleased, telling West, "It's great to have you on board." And West, who declined an interview request, was hardly done. On another Fox program, he branded [Barack] Obama's appointment of Susan Rice as national security adviser "a flip of a certain finger in the face of the American people."

Causing Controversy

The remarks set off the usual sound and fury in polarized Washington. A liberal watchdog group expressed outrage. Online sites and Twitter followers argued over the charges. And over at MSNBC's *The Ed Show*, which played a video of West's remark about Rice, liberal commentator Joy Reid declared that "the president is right to give up on negotiation with Republicans. Why? Because there is clearly no issue that Republicans in Washington won't politicize."

Nor, it often seems, is there an issue that the dueling cable channels won't hype for their own partisan purposes. Not long ago, some scholars of public discourse dreamed that an era of rapidly proliferating channels and platforms—enabling almost anyone to get airtime for their viewpoint—might soften some of democracy's rough edges by making it harder for partisans with the loudest voices and biggest signal to hijack the debate.

Instead, what was once billed as the greatest democratization of information in the world's history has helped land us where we are now. The growing personalization of media sources has yielded a world of competing commentators who, with few exceptions, stake out the rigid edge of their piece of the political spectrum. The profit is in extremity. Any remark can catch fire, and each channel or site can have outsized impact.

The result: An explosion in the availability of information has coincided with historic levels of political polarization—the starkest divide since the early 1900s, according to a Duke University study released this year. While many factors have fed this trend, analysts believe that ideological media outlets have contributed significantly and hardened the battle lines.

For some time, the hosts of some of the most popular partisan shows, such as Bill O'Reilly and Sean Hannity on Fox, Rachel Maddow on MSNBC, and Rush Limbaugh on the radio, have regularly driven the day's discussion—or at least define its extremes to left and right. They provide a forum that can gain a far larger audience than a member of Congress can get delivering a floor speech shown live on C-Span and perhaps covered by conventional news media.

The Rewards of Partisan Media

Some hosts, meanwhile, have created media empires that include paid speeches and lucrative book contracts, all of which benefit from high-octane partisanship to keep the customers coming; moderation and compromise are death on ratings.

Glenn Beck, the former Fox News host who once said that President Obama had a "a deep-seated hatred for white people," now runs an online show and has reached a distribution deal with the Dish Network. He oversees an empire with estimated revenues of $75 million last year.

"It is in the best interest of these places that partisanship keeps strong and powerful and acidic and toxic because it is more dramatic," said Robert Thompson, director of the Bleier Center for Television and Popular Culture at Syracuse University. While Thompson said it is good there are more media choices, what has been lost "is this sense we all share a certain bit of cultural glue."

In an era of shout fests, Twitter flames, and comment wars, the danger, in other words, is that the measured voice that leads to compromise has been all but drowned out.

Milking the Media

Senator Ted Cruz, the Texas Republican and Tea Party firebrand, isn't shy about saying so: He sees a boon for his cause in a media universe gerrymandered along partisan lines. Cruz went on the Rush Limbaugh show one day in late August and told the nation's top-rated talk show host about his strategy to "de-fund" President Obama's health care law. As Cruz explained to Limbaugh and millions of listeners, the strategy relied on using carefully selected, conservative-oriented segments of the media.

"Two nights ago I was on Hannity's TV show," Cruz said, referring to a Fox News program. Within two hours of that appearance, 100,000 people had logged on to a Cruz-backed website and signed a petition calling for the end of "Obamacare." With Limbaugh's help, the online signatures passed the 1-million mark. It was the broadcast prelude to the current GOP-propelled shutdown.

Limbaugh and Cruz spent part of their conversation attacking Republican leaders who dared distance themselves from Tea Party supporters. "I think they are respected less than they have been in my lifetime," Limbaugh said of the Republican leadership.

Cruz, meanwhile, shared his disdain of Obama, whom he accused of conducting a "lawless presidency."

Not long ago, a US senator like Cruz, who declined to be interviewed, would have made his case largely on the chamber floor and in nonideological, or "mainstream," media outlets. Now, just as presidents have gone over the heads of the national media, so, too, have some of the lowest-ranking members of Congress such as Cruz.

The Media Echo Chamber

Cruz took the Senate floor after his string of talk show appearances, clearly emboldened by them. He urged his colleagues on Sept. 25 to join him and "change the broken ways of Washington." The Republican-controlled House had already passed a measure defunding Obama's health care, and now Cruz wanted the Senate to do the same.

But it proved to be an exercise in fury and failure. What had sounded good in a conservative media echo chamber had no support even among most of Cruz's fellow Senate Republicans, who largely refused to stand with him.

Senator John McCain, the Arizona Republican who previously had called Cruz a "wacko bird," disputed Cruz's assertion that Republicans weren't willing to fight to kill the health care program. McCain reminded Cruz that he had campaigned for president in 2008 against the plan and lost. Mitt Romney had campaigned for repeal and lost. And now Cruz had waged his effort and lost.

Shortly after delivering his floor speech, McCain, who holds the record for the most appearances on NBC's *Meet the Press*—the very definition of a mainstream media outlet—stood in a Senate hallway and said in an interview that the rise of ideological shows is playing an outsized role in the current stalemate.

"I don't think there's any doubt that the talk show hosts, Limbaugh, Hannity, they excite their audience," McCain said. "That's their *job.*"

The voices are further amplified, McCain said, because there is "a real debate going on in the party," between isolationists and internationalists, and between the Tea Party and more traditional leaders. Ground zero of that fight has often been on the cable and radio talk shows, where McCain continues to appear regularly.

"You have to," McCain said. "To not go on these shows, I think, is just a mistake because for so many people who care a lot about the politics, this is the chance to have your political views exposed to them."

The Price

But such exposure can come with a price. Former US representative Mickey Edwards, an Oklahoma Republican, recently went on a popular talk show on which he criticized his party's increasingly rightward direction. After a rather hostile interview, the conservative host said off air, according to Edwards: "C'mon Mickey, it's just entertainment."

"The listeners don't know it is entertainment," Edwards said he responded. "They think it is straight news."

Edwards, who requested that the host's name not be revealed, said the experience left him despairing about the impact of such shows. Stressing that his concern applied equally to conservative and liberal hosts, Edwards said, "They don't understand, or they don't care, about the really toxic effect they are having on American government."

The History of Partisan Media in the United States

All of this raises the question: Why has the historic growth of media, which some believed would ratchet down discord, instead resulted in increased polarization?

In a way, it is a return to the nation's founding days. Early newspapers were openly partisan, designed to attract the most rabid followers and influence policy. But the introduction of radio in the 1920s and broadcast television in the 1950s significantly decreased polarization, according to a study coauthored by Filipe Campante, an associate professor at Harvard University's [John F.] Kennedy School of Government.

A major reason, Campante said in an interview, is that radio and broadcast television relied not on paid subscribers but on advertisers who wanted to appeal to the widest possible audience. Thus, a handful of companies that controlled major media relied on a more mainstream sensibility in their coverage.

The Fairness Doctrine

Moreover, the government had adopted a 1949 regulation that now seems quaint. The Fairness Doctrine required that "the broadcaster must be fair" to all sides and instituted the "personal attack rule," which required broadcasters to notify a person who was attacked on air, provide a transcript, and allow him or her an "opportunity to respond over the broadcaster's facilities."

The regulations, even though sporadically enforced, for years modulated the tone on the airwaves as broadcasters sought to avoid being hauled before the Federal Communications Commission.

The Rise of Senator Ted Cruz

With [Ted] Cruz's election [in 2012], he became the first Hispanic senator from Texas in American history. After his win, he talked with *CBS This Morning* about illegal immigration in the United States, saying, "I think most Americans agree, number one, that we need to get serious about securing the border and stopping the problem of illegal immigration and number two most Americans agree that we should remain a nation that celebrates legal immigrants, Americans by choice, is what Ronald Reagan said, and we need to improve our legal immigration system."

"Ted Cruz," Biography in Context.
Detroit, MI: Gale, 2012.

But the rules began to seem moot as cable television emerged. Cable channels would provide much more access to information and, because they didn't rely on public airways, weren't subject to the same regulation as broadcast venues. The Fairness Doctrine and the "personal attack rule" were killed by the administration of Ronald Reagan, which deemed them unnecessary and a violation of the First Amendment.

An Explosion of Partisan Radio

The result was dramatic. There were 100 talk radio stations in 1980, compared with 1,700 in 2007, according to a study by the liberal Center for American Progress that complained about a conservative-dominated "structural imbalance" on the radio airwaves. The most successful talk shows were hard-driving partisan affairs in which the host pushed his or her viewpoint and belittled talk of compromise.

Limbaugh, the conservative king, has the top radio show with 14 million listeners over the course of a recent week. Hannity, a conservative who also hosts a Fox prime-time program, is the second-highest-rated talk show [host] with 13.25 million listeners per week, according to Talkers.com, which tracks the ratings. Alan Colmes, who hosts a liberal show on Fox's network, has 2.75 million listeners.

The Impact of Cable Television

Meanwhile, broadcast network news viewership declined as cable installation began to bring more entertainment programs into homes, according to a study released this year by Markus Prior, an associate professor of politics at Princeton University. Millions of Americans who had only been lightly interested in politics, and had been getting "incidental" exposure to the evening news on the three broadcast networks, switched to newly available entertainment channels.

The numbers are startling. In 1980, about 52 million Americans watched the three evening network news broadcasts, compared to only 22 million people today, according to the Pew Research Center's Project for Excellence in Journalism. Cable news doesn't come close to filling the gap. For example, on Oct. 1 at the 6 p.m. hour, 2.3 million watched Fox's *Special Report*, 702,000 watched CNN's *The Situation Room*, and 811,000 watched MSNBC's *PoliticsNation*, according to ratings services. PBS said about 1 million watch its *NewsHour* program, and a scattering of other news programs attract viewers.

The bottom line: Some 25 million fewer people are watching evening news programs than in 1980, even as the nation's population has grown from 227 million to 309 million and the number of media outlets has expanded.

Many of these "lost" viewers tended to be politically moderate, and as they tuned out network news, they were less likely to track public issues and vote, according to Prior.

"The culprit turns out to be not Fox News, but ESPN, HBO, and other early cable channels that lured moderates away from the news—and the polls," Prior wrote in his study, "Media and Political Polarization." Similarly, online sites have drawn away viewers.

A Motivated Audience

At the same time, many of those drawn to the most partisan shows have an outsized impact on politics, talking to their friends and neighbors about public affairs and signing up for campaign work.

The genius of Fox News, according to Syracuse University's Thompson, was that its founders realized it could thrive without a 1980s-sized audience or centrist programming. Instead, Fox figured it could be at the top of cable news with shows watched by a couple of million viewers or less, keeping them hooked emphasizing conservative outrage. MSNBC followed suit on the liberal side, as have websites of all ideologies.

The transformation was complete.

"In the first eight decades of the 20th century we put together a consensus audience the likes of which this planet had never seen, and everybody was seeing the same thing," said Thompson. "We then spent the last two decades of the 20th century and are continuing into the 21st breaking that consensus audience into a million little pieces."

No one was more successful at profiting from this new world than Roger Ailes, a television producer and former aide to three Republican presidents, Richard Nixon, Ronald Reagan and George H.W. Bush.

> *"People tune in to partisan news because they are partisans."*

The Rise of Partisan Media Is Not Accountable for the Growing Political Polarization

Kevin Arceneaux

Kevin Arceneaux is an author and associate professor of political science, as well as the director of the Behavioral Foundations Lab, at Temple University. In the following viewpoint, he claims that it is unlikely that partisan media outlets are responsible for the unprecedented level of polarization in the US Congress. Arceneaux states that partisan media only reach a small slice of the electorate and that viewers who frequently consume partisan media are already partisan to some extent. Moreover, ideologically driven outlets emerged long after signs of political polarization were evident in the voting public and its elected representatives. Arceneaux rejects the conventional wisdom that partisan news is inherently more polarizing than mainstream news, arguing that recent evidence shows that mainstream news is just as polarizing.

As you read, consider the following questions:

1. What does the author say made partisan news possible?

2. According to Arceneaux, when did Fox News become widely available to cable television subscribers?

3. What current event story did Arceneaux and Martin Johnson use for their 2013 experiment?

In casting about for explanations for the unprecedented level of polarization in Congress, many singled out the partisan news media. This is an understandable notion, but unlikely nonetheless. Partisan media, which reach a small slice of the electorate at any rate, emerged well after Congress began to polarize, and mainstream news media have just as much power to polarize.

The expansion of programming choices on cable television in the late 1990s made partisan news media possible. But today Americans can watch not only partisan news but hundreds of other channels, most of which are not political at all, much less partisan. As Martin Johnson and I demonstrate in our new book [*Changing Minds or Changing Channels*] and discuss elsewhere, the plethora of entertainment options filters out those who are most likely to be persuaded by news shows (partisan or otherwise) and blunts the polarizing effects of partisan news on the mass public.

The Role of Partisan Media

If partisan media played any role in generating polarization in Congress, it is unlikely to have done so by polarizing the mass public first. But perhaps partisan media polarize through an indirect path. Matt Levendusky makes the case that partisan news shows energize viewers, inducing them to contact members of Congress and creating the impression of a broadly polarized electorate. While plausible, this scenario offers a better explanation for how partisan media may reinforce polarization rather than for how polarization came about in the first place.

For one, polarization in Congress precedes the advent of partisan media by almost two decades. Fox News appeared at the end of 1996 and was not widely available until the early 2000s. The parties in Congress began polarizing in the late 1970s. As Jonathan Ladd points out, it could just as easily be the case that a polarized Congress contributed to the demand for partisan news media.

Moreover, the partisan news media were relatively one-sided until the mid-2000s, when MSNBC gravitated to the left. Fox News was the first ostensibly partisan news channel on the dial, and it reported news with a conservative slant. In a working paper, Martin Johnson, René Lindstädt, Ryan Vander Wielen and I use the uneven rollout of the Fox News network to investigate its effects on congressional voting behavior. We find that *both* Democratic and Republican representatives located in districts that had access to Fox News were more likely to vote in line with the Republican agenda in the months just before the general election. This pattern is consistent with Levendusky's argument that partisan news outlets may influence elected representatives indirectly as well as the notion that representatives themselves may treat news programming as a barometer of public opinion.

But our finding undermines the claim that partisan news media generated congressional polarization: If Fox News is pushing all members to the right, it isn't polarizing them. In fact, it's entirely possible that were it not for Fox News in the 1990s, Congress would have reached today's level of polarization sooner.

What About Mainstream News

Finally, many implicitly assume that partisan news is inherently more polarizing than mainstream news. The idea here is that we are what we consume. Balanced presentations of news moderate political attitudes, while partisan presentations polarize attitudes. It is an intuitive idea but not necessarily an accurate one. People are motivated to defend cherished worldviews, especially in the realm of politics. Many studies illustrate that people are capable of cherry-picking the facts they wish to believe from balanced presentations.

In an experiment conducted in July 2013, Martin Johnson and I compared the polarizing effects of mainstream and partisan news. We asked people about their viewing habits and political predispositions and then randomly assigned them to watch either a non-political entertainment show or news story about accusations that the [Barack] Obama administration meddled in IRS [Internal Revenue Service] audits of conservative groups. Those asked to view the news story saw either one from a mainstream outlet (CBS), their side's partisan outlet (Fox for conservatives and MSNBC for liberals), or the other side's partisan outlet (Fox for liberals and MSNBC for conservatives).

A Surprising Result

After watching the program, people were asked whether the IRS audits were politically motivated or whether the IRS made an innocent mistake. The question is which program created the most polarization—that is, with conservatives taking the view that IRS audits were politically motivated and liberals taking the view that the IRS made an innocent mistake? We found that the mainstream news program was just as polarizing as the partisan news programs. Subjects assigned to view the CBS story registered more polarized opinions about the IRS than those who watched the non-political show.

What's more, the polarizing effects of both partisan and mainstream news shows were driven by the reactions of people who normally do not tune in to news programs (unless instructed to do so by political scientists, that is). In fact, partisan news viewers are more polarized than mainstream news viewers and entertainment program viewers to begin with. People tune in to partisan news because they *are* partisans. Even without partisan news media, these individuals would likely interpret the world through a partisan lens. Those who are most likely to be polarized by exposure to news—mainstream or partisan—tend to watch something else.

The rise of partisan news media is likely a symptom, not a cause, of elite polarization. Partisan media may reinforce partisan strife, but we should look elsewhere for the ultimate cause.

Periodical and Internet Sources Bibliography

The following articles have been selected to supplement the diverse views presented in this chapter.

Kevin Drum	"There's a Reason Voters Don't Blame Republicans for Congressional Gridlock," *Mother Jones*, May 16, 2014.
Gary Hart	"Gridlock and Its Causes," *Huffington Post*, May 27, 2013.
Matthew Levendusky	"Are Fox and MSNBC Polarizing America?," *Washington Post*, February 3, 2014.
Kristina D. Lorch and Jill E. Steinman	"Kennedy School Professors Discuss Causes of Congressional Gridlock," *Harvard Crimson*, November 7, 2013.
Shannon McGovern	"Who Is to Blame for Washington Gridlock?," *U.S. News & World Report*, August 23, 2012.
Marsha Shuler	"Melancon: Gerrymander Caused Gridlock in Congress," *Advocate* (Baton Rouge, LA), December 5, 2013.
Byron Tau	"Obama: Big Money Helps Cause Washington Gridlock," *Politico*, October 8, 2013.
Erik Wemple	"Obama Claims Media Are Letting GOP Off the Hook for Gridlock," *Washington Post*, May 23, 2014.
William R. Young	"Op-Ed: Inflexible Tea Party Causing Gridlock," *Stamford Advocate* (Connecticut), June 1, 2012.
Julian Zelizer	"Gridlock in Congress? Blame the GOP," CNN, May 21, 2012.

CHAPTER 3

How Should Government Gridlock Be Addressed?

Chapter Preface

The most recent example of a third-party presidential candidate having a significant impact on an election is Ralph Nader, the Green Party of the United States nominee for the 2000 election. Born in 1934, Nader had a long career as an attorney, political and environmental activist, and consumer advocate before deciding to run for president. In the late 1950s, he was thrust into the national spotlight because of his investigations into auto safety; his consumer advocacy on that issue led to a number of safety reforms, including safety belts and stronger windshields that are now standard in today's cars. During the 1970s and 1980s, he was very effective as an environmental activist, working to pass clean air and water legislation, and as an opponent to nuclear energy. By the early 1990s, there was a growing number of voices on the left calling for Nader to run for US president as a third-party candidate.

In 1996 Nader was chosen to run in the US presidential election as the Green Party candidate. Established as a national party in 1984, the platform of the Green Party espoused support of nonviolence, diversity, peace, social and economic justice, gender equality, and environmental responsibility. In the 1996 presidential election, Nader finished in fourth place, receiving only .71 percent of the national popular vote.

In 2000 the Green Party nominated Nader again. In his announcement speech, he underscored the need to put aside partisan identity and work together as Americans to take back control over American democracy and protect it from plutocrats looking to enrich the wealthiest and most powerful at the expense of the rest of the country.

In his campaign, Nader discussed a wide range of issues, including campaign finance reform, social and environmental justice, affordable housing, universal health care, increasing the minimum wage, and criminal sentencing and prison reforms. His campaign appealed to many Americans who felt that the gridlock caused by the two-party system was detrimental to the country, preventing legislators and officials from compromising and passing legislation to help the country address its most serious problems.

In the months before the election, there were calls from many Democrats for Nader to bow out of the race. They feared Nader would act as the spoiler, drawing enough votes from the Democratic candidate, Al Gore, to allow the Republican candidate, George W. Bush, to win the presidency. Nader refused to quit, stating that both candidates were equally objectionable.

In the end, the fears of many progressives, liberals, and Democrats proved valid. Although Gore did win the national popular vote, he did not win the election. It was Bush who received the most Electoral College votes: 271 to Gore's 266. Many Democrats blamed Nader for acting as a spoiler and drawing votes away from Gore, especially in the key states of Florida and New Hampshire. If Gore had won either one of these states, he would have been president.

Nader's role in the 2000 presidential election is still a point of contention today. The debate over independent and third-party candidates as a viable way to address government gridlock is one of the subjects covered in this chapter, which considers ways to remedy the problem of government gridlock. Other viewpoints in the chapter explore the possibility of changing the US Constitution, eliminating partisan redistricting, and injecting more transparency and accountability into the lawmaking process.

"Reforming winner-takes-all elections for state legislatures and Congress may be a greater challenge than upholding majority rule with runoff systems in presidential elections, but doing so is a precondition for giving all voters real choices and new voices."

A Viable Third Party Would Alleviate Government Gridlock

John B. Anderson

John B. Anderson is a former congressman who also ran as an independent presidential candidate in the 1980 presidential election. In the following viewpoint, he maintains that Americans are ready for a third-party presidential candidate who is independent of the two-party system responsible for the government gridlock paralyzing the US Congress. Anderson points to several independent candidates winning key gubernatorial and US Senate seats in the past few years. He urges Congress to reform the "winner-takes-all" electoral rules that limit third-party and in-

dependent candidates. He argues that American voters should have more choices at every level of government and should not be limited to a two-party system, especially in light of historic levels of political polarization.

As you read, consider the following questions:

1. According to Anderson, who was the major third-party candidate in the 2000 presidential election?

2. What percentage of the popular vote did Anderson get in the 1980 presidential election?

3. What law does the author say that the US Congress should repeal in order to make it easier for third-party candidates to run in elections?

We have entered another season of political discontent, with serious talk of a third-party campaign for president. Since 1968, this phenomenon has resulted in a series of independent challengers who changed campaign debate and potentially outcomes: George Wallace in 1968, my own campaign in 1980, Ross Perot in 1992, and Ralph Nader in 2000. That amounts to roughly one significant independent challenge every dozen years.

By this calendar, Americans can expect another such presidential campaign in 2012. But while it's just a matter of time before an independent wins the White House, America's "winner-takes-all" voting system suppresses potential support for independent candidates and blocks their fair representation in Congress. We need new rules better designed for the realities of today's politics.

Americans' desire for independents at all levels of government is clear. Independents and third-party candidates have won recent gubernatorial elections in Alaska, Connecticut, Maine, Minnesota, and, in 2010, Rhode Island. Last year [2010], independent candidates also finished ahead of major party nominees in races for governor and US Senate in Alaska, Colorado, Florida, and Maine.

Ross Perot's presidential candidacy in 1992 foreshadows what's possible. Mr. Perot earned 19 percent of the vote despite an erratic campaign that included leaving the race for two months. If he had instead maintained the 39 percent he polled in early June, he would have won a comfortable Electoral College majority.

Candidates today have the added benefit of our information revolution. The kind of Internet-driven self-organizing that benefited Howard Dean in 2004, Ron Paul and Barack Obama in 2008, and the Tea Party in 2010 will certainly boost a compelling independent candidate's outreach and following.

The Value of Independence

Looking to 2012, Americans can expect the Green Party [of the United States] and Libertarian [Party] to field candidates, while new groups like Ruck.us and No Labels are organizing independent-minded voters online. Americans Elect seems on its way to securing ballot access in all 50 states for an independent candidate to be chosen next spring.

Amid the stalemate in Washington and in several state legislatures, the value of independent candidates seems obvious. My own presidential campaign in 1980 provides an example of the value of more choices. With a 20-year record in Congress as a Republican able to pass legislation across party lines, paired with Patrick Lucey, the former Democratic governor of Wisconsin, as my vice-presidential candidate, I represented the kind of "unity ticket" now sought by Americans Elect.

We secured ballot access in every state and captured the imagination of millions of voters. Taking on challenges that remain difficult for the major parties to confront today, we proposed moving to end our addiction to oil with a 50-cent federal tax on gasoline and to reduce our budget deficit by making hard choices involving taxes and spending.

© Joe Heller, "Third Party," Cagle, February 23, 2010.

Independent Candidates Aren't the Real "Spoilers"

To many politicians and voters, however, I was only a "spoiler"—a candidate who is unlikely to win, but could split the majority preference for one of the major party candidates. The real spoiler is a plurality voting system that makes it possible for a presidential candidate to win all electoral votes in a state by finishing in first place, even if a majority of voters strongly oppose that candidate.

Because most states have a first-place-takes-all plurality voting system, a presidential candidate doesn't need a majority of a state's popular vote to win all of that state's electoral votes. As a result, some partisans call independent challengers like me "spoilers."

Many believe that Ralph Nader in 2000 cost Al Gore a win in the all-important state of Florida, where his vote totals dwarfed George [W.] Bush's slim lead. Similarly, in 1992, Bill Clinton won a big Electoral College majority despite winning the majority of the popular vote in only a single state—his home state of Arkansas.

Third-party candidates and independents regularly see their vote totals drop due to voters' spoiler fears. In 1980, when polls showed me falling behind Ronald Reagan and Jimmy Carter, many early backers decided to settle on the "lesser of two evils." I was blocked from the final debate and finished with 7 percent of the popular vote.

Ways to Combat Injustice of Plurality Voting

But plurality voting is not mandated in our Constitution. After my campaign, both in my work as a constitutional law professor and as board chair of FairVote, I examined other ways of electing our leaders. I identified well-tested, constitutionally sound reforms that would dramatically improve our ability to avoid the "spoiler" phenomenon in multicandidate elections for president and also provide fairer representation in elections for Congress.

To combat the injustice of plurality voting rules that we use in our presidential election, many cities, states, and nations require a separate runoff election between the top two finishers if no candidate earns a first-round majority.

A dozen cities, including Oakland, Calif., Minneapolis, Minn., and Portland, Maine, accomplish the same goal in a single election with ranked-choice voting. Voters rank candidates in order of choice, with their backup rankings allowing officials to simulate an "instant runoff" to determine the winner.

Unfair Representation in Congressional Elections

The problem of voting representation is even greater in congressional elections. It's time to take on elections that distort fair representation in our state legislatures and Congress.

By constitutional design, Congress should be responsive to all Americans, not just hard-line partisans. While majority voting can improve the democratic outcome for presidential elections, it has its disadvantages when voting for state and congressional seats. Today all state legislators and members of Congress are elected in races where a 51 percent majority in a district can elect 100 percent of representation. In other words, 49 percent of that district might support another candidate or candidates, but the candidate who wins the majority wins the district and 100 percent representation. The remaining 49 percent of voters are not accurately or fairly represented according to their real choice.

In one example, Democrats won all 10 US House races in Massachusetts in every election over the past decade even though Republicans regularly won nearly a third of the statewide vote. If voting were proportional, Republicans would have a third of Massachusetts' US House seats. But winner-takes-all elections skew representation. Democratic voters are experiencing similar futility in Midwestern states like Nebraska and Kansas.

Winner-takes-all elections in fact lock more than three in four US House races out of meaningful two-party competition, and of course fail to give a chance for third parties and independents to win fair representation. These elections utterly fail to reflect the spectrum of nuanced opinion among Americans, instead fueling partisan polarization and exaggerating the impact of money in swaying the votes of swing voters in the handful of close elections.

How to Give Voters Real Choice and Voice

Reforming winner-takes-all elections for state legislatures and Congress may be a greater challenge than upholding majority rule with runoff systems in presidential elections, but doing so is a precondition for giving all voters real choices and new voices.

As a start, Congress should repeal a 1967 law that took away the power of states to adopt proportional voting systems for US House elections. As alternatives to winner-takes-all systems, proportional voting allows like-minded voters to earn seats in proportion to their share of the vote—30 percent of the vote earns 3 of 10 seats, rather than nothing, which would be the case if their chosen candidate didn't win the most votes in their district.

As one homegrown example, from 1870 to 1980, my state of Illinois elected our state house of representatives with a proportional system called cumulative voting. Three legislators represented each district (meaning a fewer number of bigger districts), and voters could award three votes to one candidate. That simple change broke up the majority's winner-takes-all power in each district, and resulted in nearly every voter ending up with representatives from both major parties and occasionally an independent.

These reforms would make the two-party system more accountable, while allowing voters the choices they want. New technologies make them easy to implement, and their growing use in local elections demonstrates that Americans can make them work. Even if they won't be in place nationally by 2012, the only real barriers are a failure of political imagination and fear of change.

I see the coming decade as one of other major reforms, ranging from establishing a national popular vote for president, weakening the influence of special interest money in politics, and ensuring every young American is registered to vote when reaching voting age.

Given our increasingly dysfunctional government and the appeal of third-party challengers, pressure will grow on partisan dinosaurs to step aside and embrace a new politics waiting to be born: one that puts voters—and our nation—first.

> "*[With] the time so ripe for a viable third party to emerge, why does it remain so difficult for such undertakings to gain traction at any level of campaigning?*"

There Are Major Obstacles to a Viable Third Party in the United States

Scott Conroy

Scott Conroy is a political reporter for RealClearPolitics. In the following viewpoint, he investigates why a successful and lasting third-party movement in the United States has consistently failed. Conroy finds a few major obstacles: Media coverage is usually scarce for third-party candidates, unless it is a personality-driven figure such as Ross Perot; voters are skeptical about backing a third-party candidate because they don't want to "waste a vote"; and there is a substantial institutional disadvantage in the nation's winner-takes-all system, which is hostile to third-party candidates. He reviews recent mixed attempts by Americans

Elect and No Labels to identify and support independent, cen-trist candidates, arguing that these experiences show that there are still formidable obstacles to a third-party candidacy.

As you read, consider the following questions:

1. According to Conroy, in what year did Ross Perot run as an independent candidate for president?

2. How much money does the author report that Americans Elect raised?

3. According to the viewpoint, in how many states did Americans Elect gain ballot access?

For as long as the United States has maintained its two-party system of government, reformers have dreamed of upending the status quo.

From Teddy Roosevelt's Bull Moose Party [also known as the Progressive Party] of 1912 to Ross Perot's 1992 independent run for the White House, a smattering of real contenders in the last century pieced together personality-driven campaigns that threatened to change everything.

But those candidacies fell short, and time and again other efforts to establish lasting third-party movements have failed spectacularly. In next year's midterm elections [2014], just about every viable candidate on just about every ballot will have an "R" or a "D" following his or her name—a reality that persists despite polling trends indicating a large portion of the electorate views those two letters dimly; they could scarcely carry a more negative connotation if they were painted in scarlet and pinned to the candidates' chests.

And so, with the time so ripe for a viable third party to emerge, why does it remain so difficult for such undertakings to gain traction at any level of campaigning?

Obstacles to a Viable Third Party

One of the biggest impediments is a kind of catch-22: People who might consider supporting third-party candidates typically don't believe that these long shots can win, so they end up settling on a Republican or Democrat.

A similar premise applies to exposure via free media coverage: Non–major party candidates inevitably start far behind in this all-important matter.

Running in this year's Virginia gubernatorial contest as the Libertarian Party nominee, Robert Sarvis—a Harvard-educated software engineer, businessman and lawyer—hoped to capitalize on the widespread antipathy voters had for both major candidates in the race. Polling, after all, consistently showed that most voters saw choosing between Democrat Terry McAuliffe and Republican Ken Cuccinelli as akin to taking either a punch in the face or a punch in the gut.

In the end, Sarvis fared better than any non–major party gubernatorial contender in a Southern state in more than four decades. But that impressive feat was tempered by cold reality: He received only 6.5 percent of the vote and was never a threat to win.

In an interview with RealClearPolitics, he recalled crisscrossing the state in the early months of his candidacy to generate media attention and build his name identification with voters.

"The vast majority of people, they were polite about it, but you could tell it was sort of like, 'Oh, who cares?'" Sarvis recalled.

Despite the insurgent nature of his campaign and the Libertarian label that he admits evokes "a mountain guy off the grid" caricature for some, Sarvis sought to cultivate a moderate image that could appeal to all points on the ideological spectrum: He ran on a platform favoring gun rights and school choice, as well as same-sex marriage and drug policy reform.

Despite sustained warnings from the Cuccinelli camp that Sarvis was essentially acting as a stalking horse for McAuliffe, exit polls showed that the Democrat's ultimate margin of victory would have been larger had the Libertarian Party candidate not been on the ballot.

But Sarvis struggled to gain sustained media attention, even as he polled for a time in double digits. As he knew all too well, his toughest opponent wasn't McAuliffe, Cuccinelli, or the wealthy donors and interest groups that allowed each man to rack up huge sums of money.

Sarvis's most powerful foe was the American political system itself.

A Hostile System

As K. Sabeel Rahman—a Reginald Lewis Fellow at Harvard Law School—explained, candidates like Sarvis tend to do better in countries that have proportional representation, multi-member districts, or parliamentary systems, since third parties can actually win seats and gain real political power in such systems.

"Our winner-take-all electoral system is hostile terrain for viable third parties," explained Rahman, whose area of interest is democratic institutional reform. "In a system where there is only one elected representative per district, where that representative is chosen based on winning the most votes, and where the executive is elected separately from the legislature, the odds of winning actual political power are stacked in favor of big-tent parties."

In Virginia, Sarvis found that even voters who agreed with him on most issues—and preferred him on a personal level to either of the other two candidates—were reluctant to get behind him.

"Generally, it's very hard to break the mentality that you're throwing your vote away," Sarvis said. "That's the biggest thing—when people want to vote for somebody else, but they feel compelled to choose between two people who are most likely to win."

A Difficult Road

Not every third-party candidacy has been doomed to this fate. From Minnesota's Jesse Ventura to Maine's Angus King, outsiders in the recent past have achieved some success on the sub-presidential level, and there remains no shortage of interest groups who continue to promote them.

But attempts to build viable power bases—needed to galvanize the national interest and energy required to make such undertakings last—have proved futile. This track record has led most prominent reformers to conclude that a top-down approach is the most tenable solution to upending the two-party system at the presidential level.

"Any third-party movement will require someone to lead the charge," said Mark McKinnon, cofounder of the bipartisan No Labels group. "There is no question the environment is ripe for someone to step into the political vacuum. But the table stakes to get on the ballot is a minimum of $30 million. That's a huge hurdle, but not insurmountable. It just counts out most mere mortals."

McKinnon and his fellow No Labels cochairs—former Utah Gov. Jon Huntsman (a Republican) and West Virginia Sen. Joe Manchin (a Democrat)—have found avenues to voice their views on the set of MSNBC's *Morning Joe*, at high-brow think-tank forums, and during button-down symposiums around the nation's capital. But No Labels has struggled to connect beyond the David Brooks–reading set, and its focus is stuck on matters of policy and governance, not on winning the White House.

In 2010, however, a group that called itself Americans Elect set out to take a major step toward just that goal.

The group's backers were, for the most part, adherents of the socially liberal/fiscally conservative centrism professed in the pockets of money and power along the Acela corridor and on the West Coast. The group's plan was first to raise lots of money. And that's exactly what it did—hauling in an impressive $35 to $40 million, according to reports.

In that effort, Americans Elect faced intense blowback from campaign finance watchdogs for acting in the manner of a political party, but retaining a key benefit of nonprofit organizations: the ability to keep its donors anonymous.

But the ends would justify the means, or so the internal thinking went.

Next, the group launched an extensive ballot access initiative in all 50 states and an innovative, Web-based nominating process that it promised would result in a viable 2012 presidential candidate. After substantial media fanfare and gaining ballot access in 26 states, no big-name presidential contender was willing to step forward, and the group conceded defeat in May of last year, announcing that no candidate had reached its viability threshold.

The Nader Effect

Kellen Arno, who was Americans Elect's national field director, said chatter in the group's well-staffed Washington, D.C., headquarters often centered on the pitfalls of the so-called "Nader effect," a reference to Ralph Nader's third-party candidacy tipping the balance in the 2000 election to George W. Bush.

"So if I was talking to a Democrat at the time, yeah, they were frustrated with the president, but God forbid they vote for a third-party candidate and the president ends up losing because of a split vote," Arno said. "And you'd hear the exact same thing if you were talking to a Republican. So I think we're at a stage right now where people are frustrated, but they're not so frustrated that they're willing to be sort of cavalier with a vote and risk an unintended backlash."

Ross Perot

Sometimes it takes a small man to take on the Goliaths. H. Ross Perot, standing at 5 feet, 6 inches, not only took on industry giants International Business Machines [Corp.] (IBM) and General Motors Corp. (GM), but he also helped demand better treatment of U.S. prisoners of war during the Vietnam War and later led a rescue attempt to free two of his own employees held by Iranian terrorists. But one venture stands out as quite possibly the biggest of all: Early in 1992 he announced he would consider pursuing an independent . . . bid to become president of the United States. He immediately attracted enormous interest and a broad support base to seriously threaten the campaigns of Democratic Party candidate Bill Clinton and incumbent president George [H.W.] Bush—yet he never formally announced his candidacy.

"H. Ross Perot," Biography in Context. Detroit, MI: Gale, 2007.

The Challenge in Running a Third-Party Candidate

When Americans Elect began its efforts, organizers believed that gaining ballot access in all 50 states would be their biggest challenge. As it turned out, the signature-gathering process, the parameters of which are unique to each state, was indeed as onerous and costly as they imagined it would be.

But in the end, the piece of the puzzle that the group initially assumed would fall into place relatively neatly—attracting a candidate who could actually win the race—proved the most unworkable element of the entire enterprise.

"We had the money and the people to achieve 50-state ballot access," said Americans Elect CEO [chief executive officer] Kahlil Byrd. "But of all the people we briefed on this idea who would've been credible candidates, . . . they all decided not to do it. And I guess that attests to their sanity because they knew that they were going to be in a brawl with the two parties, especially if they got serious and got some traction."

The organization's fizzle came four years after a similarly minded organization, Unity08, failed to gain much interest and also collapsed.

There is a key reason, it turns out, why the last viable third-party presidential candidate was Ross Perot in 1992: He was a self-starting billionaire. In other words, the candidate came first and the organization followed. And on the presidential level, it appears that's the way it has to be.

Currently, there may be only one person with both limitless financial resources and instant national credibility who would be capable of a Perot-style campaign in 2016. And he just happens to be out of a job next month.

"If Michael Bloomberg decided today he wanted to run for president, he wouldn't lose because he couldn't get on the ballot—put it that way," Arno said.

The outgoing 71-year-old New York mayor, however, does not appear to have a presidential run on his to-do list.

Finding the Middle

But might there be some wiggle room at a different level of politics?

The Centrist Project is the latest nonprofit, 501(c)(4) group to take its shot at building an infrastructure to claim the ideological middle. The group's cofounder, Dartmouth professor Charles Wheelan, laid out his ideas for this new venture in a book published last spring, *The Centrist Manifesto*.

At the heart of this group's approach to a familiar challenge is the conclusion that previous third-party movements have aimed either too high or too low.

"What we believe is that you need to pick the right target," said Christie Findlay, the organization's executive director. "[Americans Elect] tried for president, and they also never really galvanized the country behind what they were doing. A lot of third-party projects or organizations focus on very, very local elections to build up a power base and slowly work their way up, but as a result they're spending all their time and energy focusing on super-local issues, and that's not galvanizing nationally."

Though organizers declined to provide a timeline for their goals or parameters by which success will be judged, the Centrist Project is focused on one day fielding a pragmatic-minded independent candidate who can win a U.S. Senate seat.

"The Senate is an attractive sell for people who have had success in other fields: in philanthropy, the military, industry, and the tech sector," Findlay said. "People who are executive-level innovators aren't interested in running for the House. They're not interested in running for city council, and they see the presidency as too far of a long shot. So let's start at the Senate level."

The Centrist Project is currently ramping up its fundraising arm and taking steps toward forming an offshoot super PAC [political action committee]. While it hasn't ruled out launching a candidate in next year's midterms, the project is a decidedly long-term endeavor.

Findlay brimmed with optimism about the prospect that her group may have finally cracked the third-party code, but she was also realistic when asked about the structural and institutional headwind this latest attempt will meet.

"I don't have the answer to it," she said. "If you talk to someone who does have the answer, please let me know because I think the answer is the solution to what we're facing as a country."

*"Let's have another constitutional con-
vention or at least float a few amendments to make democracy work better
in 21st-century America."*

Changing the US Constitution Would Reduce Gridlock

Ned Barnett

Ned Barnett is a reporter and editor of the News & Observer *in Raleigh, NC. In the following viewpoint, he observes that the United States should be considering bold and sweeping reforms to the way it is governed in light of the 2013 government shutdown. Barnett says one option would be to abolish the Electoral College and base elections on popular vote. Another option he posits is to change the way congressional districts are gerrymandered by taking the power away from political operators and giving it to an independent committee. Critics of reforming the US Constitution argue that the problem is more political than structural and that such big changes would not be possible with the current gridlocked US Congress. Barnett further maintains that*

Ned Barnett, "Could Constitutional Change Unlock Gridlock?," *News & Observer*, October 19, 2013. Copyright © 2013 by Ned Barnett. All rights reserved. Reproduced by permission.

another danger with changing the Constitution would be the possibility that some of the problems—the filibuster and the presidential veto—would still remain.

As you read, consider the following questions:

1. According to Barnett, after what presidential election did people want to abolish the Electoral College?

2. How did gerrymandering affect North Carolina's congressional delegation between 2010 and 2012, according to Barnett?

3. What does Barnett identify as the only hope for a productive Congress?

As gridlock gripped the U.S. Congress, the people of Ireland went to the polls to vote on a proposal many might favor here: Abolish the Senate.

The upper chamber of the Irish Parliament narrowly survived, but its brush with extinction raised the question in some minds of whether the United States also ought to be thinking of bold and sweeping changes in the way it's governed. When a divided Congress causes the government to shut down for weeks and global economic chaos looms, something in the gears of democracy needs to be fixed.

Time to Amend the Constitution?

Maybe the problem isn't really the Tea Party after all, but the firebrands who were alive during the real Boston Tea Party. Maybe we shouldn't be blaming John Boehner, Mitch McConnell and Ted Cruz, but rather James Madison, Alexander Hamilton and Ben Franklin.

I mean, Wyoming gets the same number of senators as California? Why do political operators in state capitals get to draw the U.S. congressional districts? And, for the 40th time, does the Electoral College do anything other than let the future turn on Florida chads or how Ohioans feel about gay marriage?

The pointless and costly standoff brought on by Tea Party zealots is cause to reconsider ideas hatched beneath tri-cornered hats. Let's have another constitutional convention or at least float a few amendments to make democracy work better in 21st-century America.

I played my fife and drum of exasperation and resolve for a pair of Triangle professors to see if they thought it's time to tinker with what's supposed to be a living document. The first was Michael J. Gerhardt, an expert on constitutional law at the University of North Carolina at Chapel Hill. The other was David W. Rohde, a Duke [University] political scientist who every two years since 1980 has coauthored books assessing presidential and mid-term elections.

Both wise men said my ideas to change the Constitution were as off-kilter as anything heard at a Sarah Palin rally. The fault, they said, wasn't in our Constitution, but in our politics.

A desire to change the structure of Congress is a natural response to political frustration, Gerhardt said. People also wanted to abolish the Electoral College after George [W.] Bush won the presidency in 2000 despite losing the popular vote. But he said the constitutional structure didn't fail this time. The founding fathers wanted the Senate to counter the strong feelings of the populist House and that's exactly what happened.

"The resolution of the impasse may have vindicated some of their beliefs," he said. "Senators did seem to find common ground in ways House members were unable to."

Gerrymandering

But he does think the roots of the gridlock lie partially in gerrymandered congressional districts, a result of the Constitution leaving the line drawing to the states. "It's allowed states pretty wide discretion and that's a problem," he said.

The Origins of Gerrymandering

The term *gerrymander* typically refers to the creation of electoral districts that have bizarre shapes in order to condition the outcome of an election. In "Considering the Gerrymander" (1977), Leroy C. Hardy recounts that the term *gerrymander* was coined after the Jeffersonian-controlled legislature of Massachusetts drew contorted senatorial districts in order to ensure the defeat of Federalist candidates in 1812. One particular district located north of Boston was so contorted that it was said to look like the mythical salamander. Since this all took place during Elbridge Gerry's (1744–1814) term as governor, the district was christened a "Gerrymander," and the term has stuck ever since.

"Gerrymandering,"
International Encyclopedia of the Social Sciences.
Ed. William Darity Jr. 2nd ed., vol. 3.
Detroit, MI: Macmillan Reference USA, 2008.

The problem has been compounded by the Supreme Court's silence on the matter. The court has ruled against drawing district lines to disadvantage racial groups, but it has not objected to lines drawn to enhance a political party's advantage. Thus, in North Carolina we've had Republican-led redistricting that has turned the state's congressional delegation from 7–6 Democratic in 2010 to 9–4 Republican in 2012.

Gerhardt said the most telling link between what the founding fathers did wrong and what today's Congress can't get right isn't an issue of design, but a lack of will to take on the toughest issues of their time. Those who wrote the Constitution, he said, "had some big issues like slavery, and you can see how that worked out. They kicked that can down the road and it ended in civil war. What we are learning is we can't keep kicking the can down the road."

Rohde found the idea of constitutional change amusing. In today's political climate we can't agree on changing the debt ceiling, he said, do you think we're going to agree on changing the Constitution?

Suggestions

And even if we could, should we want to? Rohde said such changes might include doing away with the filibuster, the presidential veto and making Congress one house.

"All that would make it much easier to pass laws, but it would have other impacts that people might not find so attractive," he said.

Rohde attributes the current impasse to three factors. "When we couple divided government with polarized parties with our constitutional structure we get what we've got now," he said.

And what we've got, he said, we are likely to have for a long time. For Rohde, the cause of gridlock is that the nation now has less in common politically. In the 1950s and 1960s, he said, the two major parties had a wide spectrum within each, and people from opposing parties could find partners on the other side. That's gone now and with it has gone collaboration in government.

The only hope for a productive Congress, he said, is during those periods when one party controls both chambers and the presidency. But that surge of lawmaking, he said, inevitably triggers a backlash and another round of divided and paralyzed government. "What we have experienced is what we have to look forward to for a long time," he said. "A lot of people regard that as a counsel of despair, but I can't see anything that's going to make a significant difference."

So, absent another miracle in Philadelphia, it looks like we'll be stuck between the checks and balances for awhile. But enjoy a break for the rest of the year. The next debt ceiling hike debate won't come up again until January [2014].

> "It is virtually certain that the United
> States will continue to totter unless and
> until its political leaders take strong
> steps to reestablish the institutions that
> can allow government to perform the
> few key tasks that it can do best, with-
> out intruding endlessly into the lives of
> ordinary citizens."

Changing the US Constitution Would Not Reduce Gridlock

Richard A. Epstein

*Richard A. Epstein is a senior lecturer at the University of Chi-
cago, a senior fellow at the Hoover Institution, and a professor of
law at New York University. In the following viewpoint, he rejects the idea that there needs to be serious reforms made to the
US Constitution to eliminate government gridlock. Epstein argues that gridlock has been caused by the US government's conscious deviation away from the original constitutional plan of
limited government. Instead, legislators and the Supreme Court
began a campaign to empower the federal government at the expense of the states to grow the size of federal government. He*

states that it is irresponsible to propose momentous changes in constitutional governance without any clear indication of how it will significantly improve the situation.

As you read, consider the following questions:

1. From where did Sanford Levinson take the title of his *New York Times* column, "Our Imbecilic Constitution," according to the author?

2. According to Epstein, what is the size of the federal government of GDP (gross domestic product) today?

3. How many members of the Senate and the House of Representatives does Levinson propose the president should be able to appoint during his four-year term?

The bad news about our stalled economy is distressing on two fronts. The unemployment rate recently crept back up to 8.1 percent and the stock market lost all its gain for 2012. The second reason concerns the long-term soundness of our institutions. California's fiscal crisis, for instance, is in large measure driven by its outsized pensions for retired public employees.

Sanford Levinson's Thesis

Today's problems are so pervasive, some argue, that we should rethink the fundamental structure of our venerable Constitution. University of Texas law professor Sanford Levinson's recent book, *Our Undemocratic Constitution*, argues for jettisoning our present constitutional structures in favor of more flexible institutional arrangements that, he thinks, will prove better adapted to our troubled times.

In a recent *New York Times* column, Levinson raised the ante by calling the Constitution "imbecilic." The title of his column, "Our Imbecilic Constitution," draws on the Federalist Papers' use of the epithet "imbecilic" to describe the state of affairs under the ill-fated Articles of Confederation, under which the United States suffered from a weak central government that was unable, for example, to levy taxes to support its endeavors. The federal Constitution fixed that problem by creating a stronger national government than existed under the articles, albeit one that exercised only a fraction of the powers that are now vested in Congress, some of which have been delegated to the administrative agencies. In Levinson's view, the same harsh indictment can now be made of the 1787 Constitution. His argument rests on his distaste for two principles that create gridlock: separation of powers and checks and balances. He writes:

> Our vaunted system of "separation of powers" and "checks and balances"—a legacy of the founders' mistrust of "factions"—means that we rarely have anything that can truly be described as a "government." Save for those rare instances when one party has hefty control over four branches—the House of Representatives, the Senate, the White House and the Supreme Court—gridlock threatens. Elections are increasingly meaningless, at least in terms of producing results commensurate with the challenges facing the country.

The many obstacles toward legislation, in his view, make it well-nigh impossible to form a coherent national policy.

To find a cure, Levinson argues, it is important to take a page from the progressive policies of Woodrow Wilson. Long before he was elected president, Wilson insisted that the structural safeguards of the original Constitution were an impediment to responsible social policy. Historically, it is clear that Wilson won that debate. Today's working Constitution is quite different from the sparer government regime put in place by the original Constitution, the 1791 Bill of Rights, and the Civil War amendments, most notably the Fourteenth Amendment of 1868. The Fourteenth Amendment gave citizenship to all former black slaves, and imposed extensive limitations on the powers that the states could exert over their own populations. Its net effect was to make government at both the federal and state level smaller than it had been in 1787.

The net effect of the Fourteenth Amendment was to make government smaller.

For the most part, those restrictions worked well through the early years of the twentieth century. Indeed, in writing about this issue just last week, David Brooks noted that the size of the federal government throughout the nineteenth century was about 4 percent of GDP [gross domestic product], and it grew to about 10 percent under the New Deal. According to the CBO [Congressional Budget Office] that number has increased to about 25 percent today. The increased role of the government in the economy has had a negative effect on American society: All too often, efficient private activities have been displaced by less efficient government programs with large transfer payments and high regulatory costs that do wonders for their beneficiaries but little good for anyone else.

Deviating from the US Constitution

How did we get into this position? Very simply, it was through our conscious deviations from the original constitutional plan. Historically, the overall system of limited government started to erode even before the great progressive triumphs of the New Deal era (and, most dramatically, the 1936–1937 Supreme Court term). The Seventeenth Amendment to the Constitution, adopted in 1913, authorized the direct election of senators. Before its passage, senators were chosen by state legislatures. Without question, the amendment reduced the power of the states to restrain national legislation.

The Supreme Court chipped in as well. Even though it had the power of judicial review, it did not always choose to exercise it. Between 1900 and 1920, the court gave its blessing to the progressive income tax and to estate and gift taxation. In the 1920s, it upheld New York's rent control law in *Block v. Hirsh* and extensive zoning powers in *Euclid v. Ambler*. The

1930s saw the rise of independent administrative agencies, the end of constitutional protection for economic liberties, and a vast but questionable expansion of congressional power under the commerce clause. The simple truth of the matter is that the areas in which this nation finds the greatest distress are the very areas in which federal power has expanded the most.

Throughout the 19th century, the size of the federal government was 4 percent of GDP.

Levinson's Solution for Gridlock

Levinson does not appreciate the force of these trends because he regards gridlock as a dirty word and thinks that unified government action is required to get us out of the current malaise. His suggestions are strong stuff indeed. One idea is that the winner of the 2012 presidential election gets to appoint 10 members to the Senate and 50 to the House of Representatives for his four-year term.

These numbers are not chosen at random, but are selected to give the president far greater leverage in moving through Congress whatever legislation he wants. These extra senators and representatives are, after all, not beholden to the voters in any particular state, and can thus do the bidding of the president. Levinson's idea is to introduce into the United States a parliamentary system of government through the back door, something long championed by progressives like Woodrow Wilson. Levinson suggests removing or weakening the presidential veto as part of this scheme. The point seems, however, rather idle. The president will have few occasions on which he is likely to want to veto legislation that his beefed-up party supports.

In addition, Levinson thinks that we should do away with the Electoral College; the president can thus be chosen by a popular majority. To be sure, the Electoral College has its problems. For instance, candidates don't bother to campaign in safe states. But that hardly counts as an indictment of the system. Without the Electoral College, each candidate will campaign almost exclusively in his safe states and devote far more effort in bringing out the loyal voters than in winning over-the-fence hangers. The likely result is greater nationwide polarization, especially by region. And if the election's outcome is too close to call, we would have to endure a nationwide recount that would make the *Bush v. Gore* dispute a comparative walk in the park. On this issue, it is best to leave the status quo well enough alone.

Levinson also wishes to undermine judicial supremacy. One possibility, he coyly suggests, is to require seven out of nine Supreme Court votes to overturn unconstitutional legislation. Of course, that would, in the current setting, totally insulate President Obama's health care plan from judicial assessment and effectively gut the practice of judicial review in all but the most extreme cases. Another possibility is to make Supreme Court justices responsive, in some way, to the will of the electorate, which could lead to election campaigns or recall elections on a grand scale, during which the court would still be required to function. The template for these and other unwise reforms is the pattern of governance that is found in the states, which have had little or no trouble amending their own constitutions on countless occasions.

We shouldn't take any comfort in Levinson's desire to jump from the frying pan into the fire. California has passed many constitutional amendments. It has elected judges, held recall elections, and passed popular initiatives—resulting in a set of ingrained institutional problems that threaten to heap ruin throughout the state. New York and Illinois also have lots of activity at the constitutional level, and their budgets and internal politics are in turmoil as well. The modern world offers no escape from our constitutional problems.

Today, the size of the federal government is a whopping 25 percent of GDP. . . .

Making Smart and Judicious Reforms

It is simply irresponsible to propose massive structural changes in constitutional governance without any theory to indicate why and how they are likely to improve the situation in front of us. The only way to think about governments is to first identify the set of individual rights that they are supposed to protect, after which it is possible to put in place the constitutional provisions on both individual rights and government structure that might best serve to protect those rights.

Again, David Brooks's thoughtful recounting of the role that Alexander Hamilton played in formulating a strong national government shows that the ideas of the founding period deserve to be taken seriously. Brooks rightly notes that progressives put too much faith in government planning, but he is dead wrong to think well of Wilson, FDR [Franklin Delano Roosevelt], and LBJ [Lyndon B. Johnson] for their many initiatives in regulating labor, consumer affairs, health, and education.

The expansion of government power through judicial interpretation made all these developments possible, so the Supreme Court must bear its fair share of the blame. But the root causes go deeper. Ultimately, the set of public institutions in place at the federal and state level depend critically on articulating a strong theory of rights that sufficiently limits government discretion at all levels. In my view, it is virtually certain that the United States will continue to totter unless and until its political leaders take strong steps to reestablish the institutions that can allow government to perform the few key tasks that it can do best, without intruding endlessly into the lives of ordinary citizens.

At the federal level, I have stressed over and over again that long-term tax policy should abandon progressive taxation in favor of a simpler and more stable flat tax as the sole source of revenue; the estate tax be damned. Yet, right now, every important tax rate is prey to political manipulation. Similarly, the weak protections afforded to private property and private contract allow all levels of government to use their powers of taxation and regulation to undermine private businesses for no long-term public advantage.

No one should defend a state of anarchy to ward off the excesses of state power. But unless we once again find the middle ground between too much and too little government power, we will continue to suffer as a nation, whether or not we continue to operate under what remains of the federal Constitution. The original Constitution was not imbecilic. On many questions, it reflects a level of wisdom that has unfortunately been lost today.

> "*Americans are increasingly frustrated by the disconnect between what they say they want in their government and what they see happening in Washington.*"

Can This Government Be Fixed? Three Steps That Might Help

Susan Page

Susan Page is a journalist and the Washington bureau chief for USA Today. In the following viewpoint, she maintains that one of the most effective solutions to government gridlock would be to find a way to eliminate the partisan manipulation of redistricting efforts, also known as gerrymandering. Page observes that most states allow party operators to control redistricting, resulting in congressional districts that are drawn to be overwhelmingly Republican or Democratic—depending on the party in power. In 2012 very few of the nation's congressional districts were competitive. She urges states to follow the lead of California, who recently approved an initiative to give responsibility for redistricting to an independent citizens' commission. Page suggests that two other options to address government gridlock are open primaries, in which the top two vote-getters run against each other, and filibuster reform, which would limit the practice of killing legislation by threatening endless debate.

As you read, consider the following questions:

1. According to the study cited in the viewpoint, how bad is political polarization in the United States?

2. According to the *Cook Political Report*, how many of the nation's 435 congressional districts were competitive in 2012?

3. How many cloture votes does Page report were taken in the US Congress from 2009–2010?

The third threatened government shutdown this year [2011] was narrowly averted. Congress's deficit "supercommittee" is apparently on a track to nowhere. And there has been contentious debate but little action on the proposals to help the jobless.

National Crisis

Can this government be fixed?

Americans are increasingly frustrated by the disconnect between what they say they want in their government and what they see happening in Washington. A majority want compromise; they see polarization. They want economic and other problems addressed; they see gridlock and a series of perils-of-Pauline cliffhangers. By a record 4–1 ratio in a new Gallup poll, they express dissatisfaction with the way the country is being governed.

"We are in this period of great anxiety because of economic uncertainty . . . and that has people worried about their future," says Dan Glickman, a former Democratic congress-man and cabinet secretary affiliated with the Bipartisan Policy Center. "What they need is confidence building, and what I don't think they sense from our government system is confi-dence building. Everything they see is division."

The result, he says, has "got people either nervous as hell or disengaged."

While President [Barack] Obama and congressional lead-ers wrestle over immediate crises—a stopgap deal approved by the Senate late Monday has put off the latest budget show-down until Nov. 18—a growing number of think tanks and advocacy groups with such names as No Labels, Americans Elect, Third Way and Ruck.us are trying to address underlying factors that fuel Washington's partisan stalemate.

They note three "wave" elections in a row shifted political power but failed to fundamentally change the way Washington works, or doesn't work. They have some ideas for steps that could help.

Perhaps the most significant would change the way con-gressional lines are drawn, making more districts competitive and increasing the odds that centrist candidates could prevail. Revising the rules for Senate filibusters could prevent a few senators from routinely blocking action supported by a major-ity. And changing the congressional calendar could encourage legislators to build personal relationships with colleagues from the other party.

"No one of them would turn the world upside down," William Galston, a former White House adviser now at the Brookings Institution, says of a laundry list of ideas collected in a joint study by Brookings and the Hoover Institution. "But if you did a few of them, you would probably see some changes in a relatively short period of time."

Below [are] three measures some experts say could make a government that often seems dysfunctional work better.

Drawing the Lines

The center aisle that divides Republicans and Democrats in Congress has become a chasm.

There was a time when the Democratic caucus included Southern conservatives and the Republican caucus included New England moderates, making it easier to forge bipartisan coalitions.

No more.

These days, the most conservative Democrat in the Senate, Ben Nelson of Nebraska, is more liberal than the most moderate Republican, Susan Collins of Maine. A *National Journal* study concluded political polarization is the highest in the three decades it has analyzed congressional voting patterns. The Brookings-Hoover study concluded it was the worst since the 1890s.

Gerrymandering

One reason: Many congressional districts are drawn to be overwhelmingly Republican or Democratic, in part to protect incumbents. That means one party's nominee is virtually assured of winning the general election, so the only contests that matter are the primaries—and primaries tend to be dominated by the most conservative Republican voters and the most liberal Democratic ones.

Even with the turmoil of redistricting, the nonpartisan *Cook Political Report* rates only 53 of the nation's 435 congressional districts as competitive in 2012, plus 61 more that might become competitive. In other words, control of three-fourths of the House isn't considered in question.

"As the threat to elected officials comes more from primary challenges than general election contests, the lack of cooperation seems to have become more evident and more consequential," says GOP pollster Whit Ayres, cofounder of a group called Resurgent Republic. "The people who are willing to work across the aisle and the people who are within shouting distance of the center of the political spectrum have gotten fewer and fewer."

In the wake of the 2010 census, states are redrawing congressional lines to reflect population changes. A few have launched efforts to devise districts driven more by geography than politics—likely resulting in more competitive contests and more centrist lawmakers.

"A Community of Interests"

California voters last year overwhelmingly approved a landmark initiative that turned redistricting over to a citizens' commission, charged with defining districts that share a "community of interests." Florida voters passed ballot amendments that required districts reflect existing governmental and geographical boundaries.

A few other states—including Arizona, Hawaii, Idaho, Iowa, Minnesota, New Jersey and Washington—have tried various approaches to reduce partisan manipulation of redistricting, with varying degrees of success.

They are, however, the exceptions. "The majority of states, from the perspective of most good-government reformers, are continuing to move in the wrong direction," says David Wasserman, who tracks congressional redistricting for the *Cook Report.*

Texas Republicans have drawn a map that chops Travis County among five congressional districts to divide Austin's Democratic voters and weaken an incumbent Democrat. Maryland Democrats are considering a plan that would split the state's western congressional district three ways to weaken an incumbent Republican.

Another experiment being tried in California: open primaries, in which the top two finishers run against one another in the general election, regardless of party affiliation. That could give voters the option of more centrist contenders even in sol-

The Evils of Gerrymandering

Bizarre district shape is but one manifestation of the real evil of gerrymandering: the conscious attempt by someone to organize voters in a manner that will result in the over- or underrepresentation of a particular group or political party. This can be accomplished using very unremarkable district boundaries. In addition, an electoral system can be gerrymandered by other means, such as unfairly altering the rules by which votes are counted and translated into electoral seats or changing the laws governing the qualification of candidates and political parties to appear on ballots.

Gerrymandering takes on benign as well as evil forms. Perhaps the most egregious example of modem gerrymandering in the United States took place in Alabama in 1958. The black population of the city of Tuskegee was about to become a majority of the electorate. White residents petitioned the state legislature to redraw the boundaries of the city to remove the black voters. The state legislature obliged and transformed the city's border from a simple square to what the Supreme Court of the United States described in *Gomillion v. Lightfoot* (1960) as an "uncouth" twenty-three-sided figure. The Supreme Court declared that this transformation of Tuskegee amounted to a denial of the black residents' right to vote.

"Gerrymandering,"
International Encyclopedia of the Social Sciences.
Ed. William Darity Jr. 2nd ed., vol. 3.
Detroit, MI: Macmillan Reference USA, 2008.

idly Republican or Democratic districts. Washington State adopted a similar system in 2008.

"Watch over time," says Democratic pollster Stan Greenberg, "and I think California may lead the way, as it has on some other issues." On Monday, former Phoenix mayor Paul Johnson filed papers for a ballot initiative in 2012 that would establish open primaries in Arizona.

Changing the Rules

When Tom Udall was elected to the Senate from New Mexico in 2008, he was dismayed at the difficulty of getting things moving even when most senators supported a measure.

"People want us to work with each other; they want us to put aside our differences and find common ground," he says. "But now we have an entrenched group that is very ideological, and they are putting sand in the gears."

Republicans routinely use filibusters to block action in the Democrat-controlled Senate, threatening endless debate that can only be cut off by commanding 60 votes. It is a tactic Democrats used, albeit not as often, when Republicans were in control.

What once was a rarely used maneuver has become routine. The Senate historian's office reports that cloture motions—efforts to shut off debate—rarely were filed more than a few times a year in the 19th century. That number began to expand dramatically in the 1970s and then exploded in the late 1980s.

In the last session of Congress, there were 91 cloture votes on everything from the health care overhaul to the START [Strategic Arms Reduction Treaty] nuclear treaty to a string of presidential appointments.

At the beginning of this year, Udall and several other Democratic senators offered a plan, which they said could be enacted by majority vote, aimed at reducing the number of filibusters. The proposal would have limited filibusters to final action on a bill, not to procedural motions, and would have required senators to remain on the floor during a debate designed to block a bill.

"It's like *Mr. Smith Goes to Washington*," the 1939 Frank Capra classic in which Jimmy Stewart wages a filibuster on the Senate floor, Udall says. "The core of our proposal would be to force senators to stand up and talk."

The plan won the support of 44 and 46 senators on key votes. Udall hopes to pursue the changes down the road.

"The system is broken and dysfunctional," he says, "and everyone knows that."

Meeting the Other Side

Former vice president Dick Cheney disputes those who say that Congress in some bygone day was a better, more cooperative place.

It has become "the conventional wisdom that 30 or 40 years ago times were much pleasanter in Washington; people got along; Republicans liked Democrats and so forth," he told *USA Today* in an interview about his memoir, *In My Time*. "Well, 40 years ago, when I came to town, in 1968, Martin Luther King Jr. had been assassinated; Bobby Kennedy had been assassinated; we had gone through the Tet offensive in Vietnam; we had elements of the 82nd Airborne guarding the Capitol building with machine guns. It was not a warm and fuzzy time."

The onetime congressman from Wyoming said the system "was designed for conflict."

Even so, others see changes in Washington's culture that have prevented the sort of personal relationships that can help foster a deal, or at least reduce the demonization of the other side.

"Much of the blame for the disconnect between the parties goes to the congressional calendar, where you have members scurrying home (to districts) on Wednesday nights or certainly by Thursday nights," says Matt Bennett of Third Way. "They're not around on the weekends, and the demands of fund-raising means they are separated from each other the minute the votes are over. They don't interact at all."

The centrist think tank sent an open letter to congressional leaders in January urging them to end the practice of having all the Republicans sit to one side of the House chamber and all the Democrats on the other during the State of the Union Address. Several lawmakers took the suggestion and scrambled the seating, at least for that night.

Norman Ornstein of the American Enterprise Institute, coauthor of a book that labels Congress *The Broken Branch*, suggests a schedule that would have lawmakers meet for three weeks, then take one week off to return to their districts. He'd build apartment buildings on the sites of two old hotels on Capitol Hill, rent them to members of Congress and provide child care facilities to encourage them to move families.

Ornstein also endorses an Australian law that requires citizens to vote or face a fine, guaranteeing turnout by more than activists. And the odds of that particular idea being implemented?

"Slim to none," he acknowledges, "and slim just left the building."

> *"One of the reasons why we do not have a functioning civil society in the House is that our efforts are geared towards catering to the individual member instead of focusing on our collective responsibility to govern."*

Congressional Reform and "The People's House"

John Boehner

John Boehner is the Speaker of the House of Representatives. In the following viewpoint, he acknowledges that the US Congress is paralyzed by dysfunction and gridlock, and he outlines some ways to get it functional again. Boehner proposes that members of Congress must abide by the rule of law and judiciously exercise their responsibility to negotiate budget legislation instead of ignoring the law and implementing new spending and tax increases. In addition, comprehensive spending bills should be broken up to encourage more scrutiny and better control spending. He suggests that Congress should not clamp down on open debates and should stop protecting their members from tough votes; after all, it is essentially their job to debate and make tough decisions on controversial issues. Boehner underscores the need for more transparency and accountability in order to eliminate bad legislation that does nothing to effectively address the major problems of the day.

As you read, consider the following questions:

1. According to Boehner, how much has the use of "martial law" increased?

2. How many different suspension bills does Boehner report were brought to the floor by the Democratic leader on one day in September 2010?

3. How long does Boehner say that it has been since the US Congress has reviewed its internal committee structure and eliminated duplicative programs and jurisdictions?

G ood afternoon. Thank you, Chris, for the warm welcome.

I'd like to begin by telling you a story. Some years ago back in Ohio, while I was working my way through night school at Xavier University, I started a small business. Sadly, about six months after we got up and running, my partner in the venture died suddenly. And we had one customer at the time. So there I was, with two years left at Xavier, and I was trying to hold this business together—the little bit that was still there. And, let me tell you, I fought for it with everything I had.

Looking back on it now, what strikes me is that I never thought about walking away. This was something I invested my name and my money in. And I had an obligation to that paying customer, as well as my partner who had also put his time and energy into the business.

Today, I feel the same sense of obligation and determination when I look at what's happened to our government.

Because listen, I've been here nearly twenty years, so I've seen the good, the bad, and the ugly. And lately, there's been plenty of ugly. Americans have every right to be fed up—they do. But what I won't accept—what I refuse to accept—is that we can simply walk away and let our government continue to drift—this government our forebears sacrificed everything to build.

The mission of the United States Congress is to serve the American people—and today, due in part to institutional barriers that have been in place for decades, that mission goes unfulfilled.

These wounds have been self-inflicted by both parties, and if we do not fix them, it's possible no one will. In the Constitution, the House of Representatives is the first institution of the first branch of government—the body closest to the people. That is an awesome responsibility. We should take pride in it, and be humbled by it. The House, more than any other part of our government, is the most direct voice of the people—and therefore should be afforded the most care in protecting its ability to reflect the people's will.

So today I'd like to talk to you about why this institution is broken and how we can make it function again. Because until it does, ladies and gentlemen, we don't stand a chance of addressing our deepest and most pressing problems.

Collapse of the 111th Congress

Just look at how the 111th Congress is not so much concluding as it is collapsing. Instead of tallying up a final flurry of legislative output, observers and constituents are asking, 'what went wrong?'

The answers would come easy to the people in this room, but the hard truth for families and small businesses is that their problems continue to go unaddressed.

This week, we had—in my view—an obligation to bring both parties together and stop massive tax increases scheduled to take effect on January 1st—increases we have seen coming for two years now. And, even with the existence of a clear bipartisan majority and the support of the American people, we could not get a simple up-or-down vote.

It's a sad, but not altogether surprising, finale to this Congress, and the latest in a long string of congressional sessions that have frayed the fragile bonds of trust between the American people and their legislature.

The House finds itself in a state of emergency. The institution does not function, does not deliberate, and seems incapable of acting on the will of the people. From the floor to the committee level, the integrity of the House has been compromised. The battle of ideas—the very lifeblood of the House—is virtually nonexistent.

Leaders overreach because the rules allow them to. Legislators duck their responsibilities because the rules help them to. And when the rules don't suit the majority's purposes, they are just ignored.

There's no accountability, and there are no consequences. Whether we here in Washington believe this or not, the people clearly do. Think about how our constant flouting of the rules sits with a small business owner who has to spend his or her day complying with all the mandates and regulations our government sends down.

The dysfunction in Congress is not new; both parties bear the blame for it. But the dysfunction has now reached a tipping point—a point at which none of us can credibly deny that it is having a negative impact on the people we serve. Consider:

- This is the first time since enactment of the Budget Act in 1974 that the House has not passed a budget resolution.

- This Congress is the first in our history that has not allowed one bill to be considered under an open amendment process—not one. The current freshman class has served an entire term in Congress without ever having operated under an open rule.

- And use of 'martial law'—which gives the majority the power to bring up any bill at any time and strips the minority of its few rights—has nearly doubled.

The three pillars of any democracy are the rule of law, transparency, and a functioning civil society. Over decades, all three of these pillars have been chipped away in the people's House.

The work of making our institution function again cannot be reduced to one reform or tool kit of reforms. It will require a sustained effort that rests on the three pillars and firmly adheres to the job description laid out in Article I of the Constitution.

Rule of Law

First, the rule of law. We always hear members of Congress talking about swearing an oath to represent their constituents when in reality the only oath we take is to the Constitution. We pledge "to support and defend the Constitution of the United States." No more, no less.

But we have strayed far afield from our job description. Members go out and promise their constituents the moon, and to try and fulfill those commitments, they agree to conform to a system that emphasizes seniority and party loyalty. The ropes they are shown lead to passing more bills, micromanaging more bureaucracies, and raiding the federal treasury.

That is why, in the Pledge to America, the governing agenda my colleagues and I issued last week, we state that every bill that comes to the floor of the House should contain a clear citation of constitutional authority. If we cannot do this much—we should put down the pen and stop right there.

Congress has been most maligned over the past generation for its fiscal recklessness, and rightly so. Mindful of the dangers of 'taxation without representation,' the framers handed the power to tax and spend to the legislative branch exclusively. It's right there in Article I, Section 9.

But having the right to do something doesn't necessarily make it the right thing to do. Current congressional rules are rigged to make it easy to increase spending and next to impossible to cut spending. Much of the law that governs the process—the Budget Act of 1974—is tied to rules instead of statutes. Consequently, we routinely waive the Budget Act's requirements to serve our purposes. Can't write a budget? Just waive the rule and move on. No harm, no foul. The "pay as you go" rule has been repeatedly ignored to justify billions of dollars in new spending and tax and fee increases. So we ought to start at square one and give serious consideration to revisiting, and perhaps rewriting, the 1974 Budget Act.

While the culture of spending stems largely from a lack of political will in both parties to say 'no,' it is also the consequence of what I believe to be a structural problem. As Kevin McCarthy often says, structure dictates behavior. Aided by a structure that facilitates spending increases and discourages spending cuts, the inertia in Washington is currently to spend—and spend—and spend. Most spending bills come to the floor prepackaged in a manner that makes it as easy as possible to advance government spending and programs, and as difficult as possible to make cuts.

Again, this is not a new problem. But if we're serious about confronting the challenges that lie ahead for our nation, it's totally inadequate.

I propose today a different approach. Let's do away with the concept of "comprehensive" spending bills. Let's break them up, to encourage scrutiny, and make spending cuts easier. Rather than pairing agencies and departments together, let them come to the House floor individually, to be judged on their own merit. Members shouldn't have to vote for big spending increases at the Labor Department in order to fund Health and Human Services. Members shouldn't have to vote for big increases at the Commerce Department just because they support NASA. Each department and agency should justify itself each year to the full House and Senate, and be judged on its own.

For decades, the word "comprehensive" has been used as a positive adjective in Washington. I would respectfully submit that those days are behind us. The American people are not well served by "comprehensive." In an era of trillion-dollar deficits, we need a tighter focus; one that places an emphasis on getting it right, and less emphasis on getting it done quickly.

Don't assume I'm singling out the appropriators; I'm not. Over decades, in my view, authorizing committees in the House and Senate have also abdicated their responsibility, often authorizing billions of dollars knowing full well they will never actually be appropriated. Interest groups then lobby Congress to "fully fund" the program, systematically creating pressure on the legislature to drive up spending. This has to stop. Authorizing committees should be held to the same standard as the appropriations committee: authorize what we can afford, and hold agencies to account for results.

We should also consider developing a "cut as you go" rule that would apply to any member proposing the creation of new government programs or benefits. Very simply, under this "CutGO" rule, if it is your intention to create a new government program, you must also terminate or reduce spending on an existing government program of equal or greater size—in the very same bill.

Just this week, the majority leadership brought 85 different suspension bills to the floor on a single day—many of them creating new government programs, some of which had been subject to little if any scrutiny or debate. If we'd had a "CutGO" rule in place this week, roughly half of these 85 bills would never have made it to the floor.

CutGO was conceived by my friend and colleague Roy Blunt. And as he put it, 'let's turn the activists for big government on each other, instead of letting them gang up on the taxpayer.' Through this public discussion, we might end up finding out that neither program has a whole lot of merit in the first place. It may sound simplistic, but sometimes that's the best place to start.

Of course, no amount of spending control can substitute for the critical role of oversight. We should direct every committee to make its oversight responsibilities a top priority, and to make no apologies for it. Both parties should work together to ensure each program is meeting congressional intent and serving the national interest. Republicans should not start from the assumption that all government is bad; nor should Democrats start from the assumption that all government is good. Oversight should be conducted by uniform standards:

- What's the purpose of this program?

- What's its responsibility?

- Is this the best use of taxpayers' time and money?

Of course, if we're truly serious about being responsible again on spending, we need to do something about earmarks.

As we know too well, earmarks are the often-questionable spending projects that are slipped into bills with little scrutiny. They run the gamut from bridges to nowhere and "monuments to me" to sewer projects and art exhibits. They ride on authorizing bills, appropriations bills, and tax bills. An entire lobbying industry has been created around them. And they've become a symbol of a spending process that has broken faith with the American people.

House Republicans voted to stop the process this year—on our own, without cooperation from Democrats—so that we could begin reforming how Washington spends taxpayers' money.

Like the decision to adopt the moratorium in the first place, the future of the moratorium will be a collective decision, made by our members. But on the question of earmarking, my colleagues and my constituents know where I stand. I told my constituents in 1990: if you believe it's important to have a representative who will go to Washington and raid the federal treasury on your behalf, you should probably vote for someone else. I've had a personal 'no earmarks' policy since I began serving in Congress, and I always will. I believe it is our obligation to end earmarking as we know it and bring fundamental change to the manner in which Washington spends taxpayers' money, and I will continue to be an advocate for reforms to ensure that happens.

Functioning Civil Society

One of the reasons why we do not have a functioning civil society in the House is that our efforts are geared towards catering to the individual member instead of focusing on our collective responsibility to govern. The rules are too often manipulated to shut down debate and protect individual members from tough votes.

In recent years—and not just under the current majority—the minority has been forced to use the motion to recommit, often in ways that are painful for the majority, to ensure the minority's voice is heard. And in turn, the majority has responded by conjuring up new ways to shut the minority out even further. It's a cycle of gridlock.

Here's my question: What are we so afraid of?

The more we do to avoid risk and protect our members from tough votes, the more ineffective and polarized the institution becomes. The House was designed to reflect our natural contentiousness as a people. That's the genius of our system.

So instead of clamping down even further, it's my view that we should open things up and let the battle of ideas help break down the scar tissue between the two parties. Yes, we will still have disagreements. But let's have them out in the open. Yes, we will still try to outmaneuver each other. But let's make it a fair fight. Instead of selling our members short, let's give them a chance to do their jobs. Let's let legislators legislate again.

Again, structure dictates behavior. More debate and more amendments will mean more intense scrutiny, and ultimately, better legislation.

Just as we've shielded members from tough votes, we've also enabled them to write bad bills. With all the challenges facing our nation, it is absurd that Congress spends so much time on naming post offices, congratulating sports teams, and celebrating the birthdays of historical figures.

Now, I know the drill: Members get good press opportunities back home and leaders get cover while stalling on the people's priorities. But often these resolutions are poorly drafted, or duplicative of previously considered bills. And under both parties they've received little or no oversight. It's my view that we should consider taking all these commemorative moments and special honors, and handle them during special orders and one-minute speeches. It's time to focus on doing what we were sent here to do.

The ultimate measure of whether we have a functioning House is not bipartisanship. Our focus shouldn't be on working across party lines for its own sake. The true test is whether our ideas, policies, and values are able to stand the test of a fair debate and a fair vote. And sadly, that's something we have not seen in the House for some time.

The Rise of John Boehner

John A. Boehner won a tight race to become majority leader in the U.S. House of Representatives in early 2006. The Ohio Republican succeeded his ousted House colleague, Tom DeLay, as holder of one of the most powerful positions in Washington. When the Republicans lost their majority in Congress in the November 2006 midterm elections, Boehner was elected by his colleagues as Republican leader in the House of Representatives for the coming term. In 2010 the Republicans regained control of the House, and Boehner was elected the Speaker of the House.

"John A. Boehner," Biography in Context.
Detroit, MI: Gale, 2013.

Transparency

Of course, it's hard to guarantee a fair debate when the majority has the ability to change bills in the dark of night and literally drop them into the laps of the minority just hours before debate is set to start. Without transparency, lawmakers cannot hold each other accountable, and the American people cannot hold us to account.

That's why in the Pledge to America we say that the text of all bills should be published online for at least three days before coming up for a vote. No exceptions. No excuses.

But this lack of transparency speaks to a larger problem where the Speaker's office has the capacity to unilaterally draft a bill and send it straight through to the Rules Committee.

Woodrow Wilson once said that 'Congress in session is Congress on public exhibition, while Congress in its committee rooms is Congress at work.' If President Wilson went from committee room to committee room today, he might take that statement back. Because the truth is, much of the work of committees has been co-opted by the leadership. In too many instances, we no longer have legislators; we just have voters.

In my view, if we want to make legislators legislate again, then we need to empower them at the committee level. If members were more engaged in their committee work, they would be more invested in the final products that come to the floor.

From 2001 to 2006, I had the privilege to serve as chairman of the Education & the Workforce committee. The ranking member at the time was George Miller of California. Now, no one would confuse me and George Miller for ideological soulmates. But in just a few years, we were able to work together to transform our committee from a "backwater" panel that nobody wanted to be on to an active panel at the center of some of the biggest issues of the day. By focusing on our work, letting our members be legislators, and setting high standards, we were able to elevate the committee to its proper role. There's no reason every single committee in the House can't achieve the same thing.

Much of this is up to committee chairmen and ranking members themselves. If every chairman and ranking member started with the mind-set that their committee's bill could be the one that comes to the floor, better legislation would result. Chairmen shouldn't be content to churn out flawed bills and then rely on their leadership to bail them out. Chairmen should operate with the assumption that their bills are going to be on the floor, and assume that once their bills are on the floor, they'll be subject to an open rule. If all committee chairmen and ranking members had this mentality, the result would be better legislation, and better legislators.

At Education & the Workforce, we operated with a set of transparency rules that encouraged deliberation and limited problems:

- First, we gave at least three days' notice on all bills. Actually, we normally went above and beyond this standard, giving about a week's notice on each bill, but three days was the rule. That gave members plenty of time to gain an appropriate depth of knowledge and scrub each bill for potential land mines.

- We also required that all votes be posted online within 48 hours of being cast. Believe it or not, committees are not currently required to post these records at all, let alone within a certain time frame. If we posted these records online, more members would be inclined to do their jobs, attend committee proceedings, and weigh in on a bill before it goes to the floor.

- And third, any amendments had to be posted online within 24 hours after being adopted. We have seen in the past instances where 'phantom amendments' are made to bills in committee after being voted on without any accountability whatsoever. That's not acceptable.

We should require that all committees meet these standards. We should also require that all committees—especially the Rules Committee—webcast their proceedings and post complete transcripts online—with obvious exceptions for those panels dealing with state secrets and classified information.

To ensure there is proper oversight, Congress should also review its internal committee structure and eliminate duplicative programs and jurisdictions. This hasn't been done in 15 years. Think about that. We can't ask members to become more engaged if they sit on three different committees and more than a handful of subcommittees. We currently have rules regarding member limitations, but of course they're frequently waived to have warm bodies in those slots. We need to rethink that.

An Ongoing and Inclusive Effort

I know I've covered a lot of ground here, and thrown out a lot of ideas. Some of them may get off the ground in the next Congress; others may not. But it's vital that we have the discussion, and equally vital that the discussion starts now.

Reform should be an ongoing and inclusive effort. I don't have all the answers, and wouldn't pretend to. I welcome ideas and helping hands from any lawmaker or citizen about how we can make this institution function again.

Americans who long for a better government must continue to speak out. And when they do, we have to listen.

The People's House

Don't confuse my enthusiasm for any illusion about how well these reforms will be received. I can remember early on in my career, as a member of the 'Gang of Seven,' how I would get long stares from members—many of them in my own party. Some would walk the other way. Some would put themselves directly in my face.

That's probably the reaction I'll get to some of the things I've talked about here today. But some changes have to be made, and we can't keep kicking the can down the road. We've run out of road.

It's time to do what we say we're going to do. For our constituents, our government, and the people's House, settling for the "next best thing" is no longer good enough.

Exactly one hundred years ago, Uncle Joe Cannon—who ruled the House with an iron fist—faced a revolt from insurgent Republicans and Democrats. Even though his fall from power was imminent, Speaker Cannon refused to resign, calling it a 'confession of weakness or mistake or an apology.'

That right there was Cannon's mistake. That gavel, those powers—they weren't his to use as a personal guard or shield. They were given to him to guard and shield the interests of the American people.

So the Speakership foundered over the next decade, until late 1925, when Nick Longworth told the House on the day he was sworn in: 'I want to effectively assist you in bringing about universal recognition of the fact that this House, closer as it is to the people than any similar body and more directly responsive to their will, is in very truth, as it ought to be, the most dominant legislative assembly in the world.'

Let that be our goal: a people's House that is quiet in its effectiveness, but unmistakable in its pride and purpose.

We should pursue this work as if the future of the institution depended on it—because it does.

Thank you for having me. I look forward to taking your questions.

Periodical and Internet Sources Bibliography

The following articles have been selected to supplement the diverse views presented in this chapter.

Eric Black   "If You're Sick of Gridlock, Blame the Constitution," *Huffington Post*, October 1, 2012.

Boston Herald   "Snowe to Help Unveil Reforms for Ending Gridlock," June 23, 2014.

Alanna Durkin   "Bipartisan Group Offers Proposal to End Gridlock," Salon.com, June 24, 2014.

Economist   "Political Gridlock: Intransigence Is Good Strategy," March 20, 2014.

Joseph J. Ellis   "Could the Founding Fathers Solve Today's Political Gridlock?," *Los Angeles Times*, February 21, 2014.

William Freeland   "Political Gridlock Shouldn't Be Solved with Monarchy," *Daily Caller*, December 23, 2013.

William A. Galston   "Four-Year House Terms Would End the Gridlock," *Wall Street Journal*, February 25, 2014.

Courtney E. Martin   "Breaking Partisan Gridlock over a Cup of Tea," Al Jazeera, September 25, 2013.

Max Nisen   "Four Smart Ways to Reduce US Political Gridlock, Our Biggest Economic Problem," *Business Insider*, July 25, 2012.

Peter Orszag   "Too Much of a Good Thing," *New Republic*, September 14, 2011.

PBS NewsHour   "Would a Third Major Party Ease Congressional Gridlock?," October 13, 2013.

OPPOSING
VIEWPOINTS®
SERIES

CHAPTER 4

How Will Filibuster Reform Impact Government Gridlock?

Chapter Preface

On November 21, 2013, Senate majority leader Harry Reid announced his proposal to change the way the US Senate could confirm candidates who were nominated for judicial and executive branch positions by the US president. Reid's proposal would end the use of the filibuster, a parliamentary device used by legislators to prevent votes on bills or confirmations from coming to the floor without the approval of sixty senators (out of one hundred). The only exception to the reform would be nominees for the US Supreme Court. The filibuster could still be used to block most legislation, according to existing Senate rules.

For years before Reid's announcement, legislators, political commentators, and the media debated the merits of filibuster reform. Supporters of the proposal argued that Republicans were abusing the tactic, citing the increasingly frequent use of the filibuster to block President Barack Obama's nominees to cabinet and judicial positions. As of November 2013, there were fifty-nine executive branch nominees and seventeen judicial branch nominees awaiting confirmation. Some candidates had been waiting for months to go through the confirmation process.

In his announcement, Reid stated his belief that Republicans were increasingly abusing the filibuster, especially in regard to the confirmation process. "In the history of the Republic, there have been 168 filibusters of executive and judicial nominations," he observed. "Half of them have occurred during the Obama administration—during the last four and a half years. These nominees deserve at least an up-or-down vote. But Republican filibusters deny them a fair vote and deny the president his team. This gridlock has consequences. Terrible consequences. It is not only bad for President Obama and bad for the United States Senate; it's bad for our country."

Critics of filibuster reform denounced the proposed change as politically motivated to make it harder for the minority party to offer amendments or allow sufficient debate on issues and nominees. Republican leaders deemed it a cynical power grab, a move made for short-term advantage at the expense of the Senate's long-standing role as a check against radical nominees being appointed to key roles in the president's administration or as judges on a top federal court.

In his response to Reid's proposal, Senate minority leader Mitch McConnell expressed his frustration, warning Democrats that Republicans would be sure to use filibuster reform to their advantage when they were in power. "Let me assure you: This Pandora's box, once opened, will be utilized again and again by future majorities—and it will make the meaningful consensus-building that has served our nation so well a relic of the past. . . . They're not interested in checks and balances. They're not interested in advice and consent. They're not even interested in what this would mean down the road when Republicans are the ones making the nominations. They want the power. They want it now. And they don't care about the consequences."

On November 21, 2013, the Senate voted on Reid's proposal for limited filibuster reform. The members voted fifty-two to forty-eight to approve the rule change.

The question of how filibuster reform will impact the problem of government gridlock is the subject of this chapter. The following viewpoints debate which political party will get a long-term advantage because of filibuster reform, the dangers of changing the Senate rules and bucking long-standing tradition, and the need for reform in order to keep the Senate from becoming an obsolete and even more ineffective government body.

| *"It's time to change the Senate, before this institution becomes obsolete."*

There Needs to Be Filibuster Reform to Maintain a Functioning Democracy

Harry Reid

Harry Reid is a US senator from Nevada and was the Senate majority leader until January 2015, when he became minority leader. In the following viewpoint, he criticizes the historic levels of government gridlock in the current Congress, observing that dysfunction and political polarization have paralyzed the body and prevent lawmakers from effectively addressing the nation's major problems. A result of congressional gridlock is that the executive and judicial branches are hobbled by vacancies because of stalled confirmation votes on qualified nominees. Reid points out that the consequences are detrimental to national security and the economic health of the nation. Therefore, filibuster reform is essential to lessen gridlock and to get Congress working efficiently again. He proposes that executive and judicial nomi-

Harry Reid, "Speech on Filibuster Reform," November 21, 2013. http://talking pointsmemo.com/livewire/read-harry-reid-s-full-speech-calling-for-filibuster-reform.

nees get an up-or-down vote on confirmation in the Senate. He believes this is a commonsense reform that will allow the Senate to meet the challenges of modern society.

As you read, consider the following questions:

1. According to Reid, how many filibusters of executive and judicial nominations have there been in the history of the United States as of November 2013?

2. How long does Reid say that Defense Secretary Chuck Hagel's nomination was pending in the Senate?

3. What percentage of the DC Circuit does Reid report is vacant?

The American people believe Congress is broken. The American people believe the Senate is broken. And I believe the American people are right.

A Historical Level of Dysfunction

During this Congress—the 113th Congress—the United States Senate has wasted an unprecedented amount of time on procedural hurdles and partisan obstruction. As a result, the work of this country goes undone. Congress should be passing legislation that strengthens our economy and protects American families. Instead we're burning wasted hours and wasted days between filibusters.

Even one of the Senate's most basic duties—confirmation of presidential nominees—has become completely unworkable. For the first time in history, Republicans have routinely used the filibuster to prevent President [Barack] Obama from appointing his executive team or confirming judges.

It is a troubling trend that Republicans are willing to block executive branch nominees even when they have no objection to the qualifications of the nominee. Instead, they block qualified executive branch nominees to circumvent the legislative process. They block qualified executive branch nominees to force wholesale changes to laws. They block qualified executive branch nominees to restructure entire executive branch departments. And they block qualified judicial nominees because they don't want President Obama to appoint any judges to certain courts.

The need for change is obvious. In the history of the Republic, there have been 168 filibusters of executive and judicial nominations. Half of them have occurred during the Obama administration—during the last four and a half years. These nominees deserve at least an up-or-down vote. But Republican filibusters deny them a fair vote and deny the president his team.

Dire Consequences

This gridlock has consequences. Terrible consequences. It is not only bad for President Obama and bad for the United States Senate; it's bad for our country. It is bad for our national security and for our economic security.

That's why it's time to get the Senate working again—not for the good of the current Democratic majority or some future Republican majority, but for the good of the country. It's time to change the Senate, before this institution becomes obsolete.

At the beginning of this Congress, the Republican leader pledged that, quote, "this Congress should be more bipartisan than the last Congress." We're told in scripture that, "When a man makes a vow . . . he must not break his word," Numbers 30–2. In January [2013], Republicans promised to work with the majority to process nominations . . . in a timely manner by unanimous consent, except in extraordinary circumstances.

Exactly three weeks later, Republicans mounted a first-in-history filibuster of a highly qualified nominee for secretary of defense. Despite being a former Republican senator and a decorated war hero, Defense Secretary Chuck Hagel's nomination was pending in the Senate for a record 34 days, more than three times the previous average. Remember, our country was at war. Republicans have blocked executive branch nominees like Secretary Hagel not because they object to the qualifications of the nominee, but simply because they seek to undermine the very government in which they were elected to serve.

The Laws of the Land

Take the nomination of Richard Cordray to lead the Consumer Financial Protection Bureau. There was no doubt about Mr. Cordray's ability to do the job. But the Consumer Financial Protection Bureau—the brainchild of Senator Elizabeth Warren—went for more than two years without a leader, because Republicans refused to accept the law of the land—because they wanted to roll back a law that protects consumers from the greed of big Wall Street banks. I say to my Republican colleagues, you don't have to like the laws of the land. But you do have to respect those laws, acknowledge them and abide by them.

Similar obstruction continued unabated for seven more months, until Democrats threatened to change Senate rules to allow up-or-down votes on executive nominees. In July, after obstructing dozens of executive nominees for months, and some for years, Republicans once again promised that they would end their unprecedented obstruction.

One look at the Senate's executive calendar shows nothing has changed since July. Republicans have continued their record obstruction as if no agreement had ever been reached. Republicans have continued their record obstruction as if no vow had ever been made. There are currently 75 executive branch nominees ready to be confirmed by the Senate that have been waiting an average of 140 days for confirmation. One executive nominee to the agency that safeguards the wa-

Senator Harry Reid

When Harry Reid was chosen U.S. Senate majority leader, the Democrats had just come off reclaiming both houses of Congress in a midterm election. But in his inaugural speech in January of 2007 as majority leader, Reid stressed bipartisan cooperation. "The majority my party holds is slim: 51–49," Reid said, as quoted in the *Washington Times*. "Some may look at this composition as a recipe for gridlock, but I see it as a unique opportunity—an opportunity for Democrats and Republicans to debate our differences and seek common ground."

"Harry Reid," Biography in Context. Detroit, MI: Gale, 2014.

ter our children and grandchildren drink and the air they breathe has waited more than 800 days for confirmation.

We agreed in July that the Senate should be confirming nominees to ensure the proper functioning of government. But consistent and unprecedented obstruction by the Republican caucus has turned "advise and consent" into "deny and obstruct."

Filibuster Abuse

In addition to filibustering a nominee for secretary of defense for the first time in history, Senate Republicans also blocked a sitting member of Congress from an administration position for the first time since 1843. As a senior member of the House [Committee on] Financial Services, Congressman Mel Watt's understanding of the mistakes that led to the housing crisis made him uniquely qualified to serve as administrator of the Federal Housing Finance Agency. Senate Republicans simply don't like the consumer protections Congressman Watt was nominated to develop and implement. So they denied a fellow member of Congress and a graduate of Yale Law School even the courtesy of an up-or-down vote.

In the last three weeks alone, Republicans have blocked up-or-down votes on three highly qualified nominees to the D.C. Circuit Court of Appeals [formally known as the United States Court of Appeals for the District of Columbia Circuit], considered by many to be the second highest court in the land. Republicans have blocked four of President Obama's five nominees to the D.C. Circuit, whereas Democrats approved four of President [George W.] Bush's six nominees to this important court. Today, 25 percent of the D.C. Circuit Court is vacant. There isn't a single legitimate objection to the qualifications of any of these nominees. Yet Republicans refused to give them an up-or-down vote—a simple yes-or-no vote. Republicans simply don't want President Obama to make any appointments at all to this vital court.

Further, only 23 district court nominees have been filibustered in the entire history of this country. Twenty of them were nominated by President Obama. With one out of every 10 federal judgeships vacant, millions of Americans who rely on courts that are overworked and understaffed are being denied the justice they rightly deserve. More than half the nation's population lives in a part of the country that's been declared a "judicial emergency."

Reform Proposals

The American people are fed up with this kind of obstruction and gridlock. The American people—Democrats, Republicans and independents—are fed up with this kind of obstruction and gridlock. The American people want Washington to work for American families once again.

I am on their side, which is why I propose an important change to the rules of the United States Senate. The present Republican leader himself said, "The Senate has repeatedly

181

changed its rules as circumstances dictate." He is right. In fact, the Senate has changed its rules 18 times by sustaining or overturning the ruling of the presiding officer in the last 36 years, during the tenures of both Republican and Democratic majorities.

The change we propose today would ensure executive and judicial nominees get an up-or-down vote on confirmation— yes or no. This rule change will make cloture for all nominations other than Supreme Court nominees a majority threshold vote—yes or no.

The Senate is a living thing. And to survive, it must change. To the average American, adapting the rules to make Congress work again is just common sense. This is not about Democrats versus Republicans. This is about making Washington work—regardless of who's in the White House or who controls the Senate. To remain relevant and effective as an institution, the Senate must evolve to meet the challenges of a modern era.

I have no doubt my Republican colleague will argue the fault lies with Democrats. I can say from experience that no one's hands are entirely clean on this issue. But today the important distinction is not between Democrats and Republicans. It is between those who are willing to help break the gridlock in Washington and those who defend the status quo.

Today Democrats and independents are saying enough is enough. This change to the rules regarding presidential nominees will apply equally to both parties. When Republicans are in power, these changes will apply to them as well. That's simple fairness. And it's something both sides should be willing to live with to make Washington work again.

> *"Allowing majority rule to always trump minority interests would undercut the intent and structure of the Constitution, with its many protections of minorities from the tyranny of majorities."*

Filibuster Reform Is a Shortsighted and Dangerous Solution to the Problem of Gridlock

John Samples

John Samples is an author and the director of the Center for Representative Government at the Cato Institute. In the following viewpoint, he urges Democratic leaders to reconsider filibuster reform, arguing that the filibuster is a vital tool for the minority party to stifle bad legislation based on the tyranny of the majority. Samples points out that the filibuster allows minority interests to be represented and often forces lawmakers to compromise in order to pass legislation. The filibuster also opens up de-

bate and enhances accountability in the legislative process. He concludes that reforming the filibuster is a risky and shortsighted solution to the problem of party gridlock in the US Senate.

As you read, consider the following questions:

1. According to Samples, how many votes are required under the Senate's cloture rule to stop debate and require a vote?

2. According to the viewpoint, how many justices are on the US Supreme Court?

3. Why is Samples surprised that some Democrats are now so willing to jettison the filibuster?

The U.S. Senate has long promised and tolerated unlimited debate on legislation. It's only with 60 votes that the Senate's "cloture" rule can be invoked to stop debate and require a vote. In practice, that means that 41 senators can block most action by threatening to prolong debate, or filibuster. But now some senators and outside interests want to allow debate to be cut off by a simple majority, eliminating the filibuster.

The desire for change comes from partisan passions and recent frustrations. During President [Barack] Obama's first term, the Senate's Republican minority used the filibuster to modify laws passed by the Democratic-controlled House. The 2009 "stimulus" bill spent less than it would have under strict majority rule, and the health care overhaul might well have included a public option if not for the filibuster.

The Tyranny of Majority Rule

Past partisan frustrations, however, should not determine future legislative rules. Allowing majority rule to always trump minority interests would undercut the intent and structure of the Constitution, with its many protections of minorities from the tyranny of majorities.

What Is the Filibuster?

The filibuster is widely viewed as one of the Senate's most distinctive procedural features. Today, the term is most often used to refer to senators holding the floor in extended debate. More generally, however, "filibustering" includes any tactics aimed at blocking a measure by preventing it from coming to a vote.

As a consequence, the Senate has no specific "rules for filibustering." Instead, possibilities for filibustering exist because Senate rules deliberately *lack* provisions that would place specific limits on senators' rights and opportunities in the legislative process. In particular, those rules establish no generally applicable limits on the length of debate, nor any motions by which a majority could vote to bring a debate to an end, or even limit it.

The only Senate rule that permits the body, by vote, to bring consideration of a matter to an end is . . . known as the "cloture rule." Invoking cloture requires a supermajority vote (usually 60 out of 100 senators), and doing so does not terminate consideration, but in most cases only imposes a time limit. Cloture also imposes restrictions on certain other potentially dilatory procedures. In recent years, as a result, cloture has increasingly been used to overcome filibusters being conducted not only by debate, but through various other delaying tactics.

Richard S. Beth and Valerie Heitshusen,
"Filibusters and Cloture in the Senate,"
Congressional Research Service, May 31, 2013.

In general, the American Constitution does not set up government by majorities. The nine members of the Supreme Court interpret and enforce the Constitution, and they are neither selected by nor responsible to a majority. Simple majority rule does not make laws, either, and not just because of the filibuster. Legislation must be approved by three institutions, each representing different constituencies.

Majority rule is not the norm in American politics, nor should it be. To see why, consider an institution that is ruled by the majority: the House of Representatives. For years, both Republican and Democratic minorities in the House have complained about being shut out of debates and precluded from offering amendments.

As political scientist Gregory Koger has noted, the filibuster has been used to force Senate majorities to consider minority amendments. A majority has every reason to prevent such amendments; they often force senators in the majority to cast tough votes on controversial issues. By forcing amendments, however, the filibuster enhances accountability while expanding the scope of the debate.

While the House is organized along partisan lines, the Senate is much more individualist, partly because of the filibuster. Getting rid of the filibuster would increase the power of party leaders. Will senators represent their states better if they are more at the mercy of party leaders? In a polarized age, do we really need more partisanship in the Senate?

Polarization has left both parties with fewer members from the political center. Simple majorities in the Senate would be more likely to endorse laws that are far from the center. The current threat of filibusters requires the majority party to move toward the center, satisfying more voters. In a polarized time, the filibuster tends to make Senate actions more representative of the nation as a whole.

The Benefits of Gridlock

Of course, the prospect of filibusters often prevents laws from passing. But it's far from clear that laws reflecting a partisan agenda are preferable to inaction.

It's surprising that some Democrats are now so willing to jettison the filibuster. Did they not use it during George W. Bush's administration? Do they expect to hold the Senate majority forever? The Democrats cannot hope to end the filibuster now and then reinstate it if the Senate goes Republican in 2014—at which point we might expect the GOP to discover the advantages of unhampered majority rule.

Some have observed that the proponents of ending the filibuster are relatively new to the Senate and may not understand how it benefits both parties and the nation. Since both parties (and their voters) will be in the minority at one time or another, the filibuster serves broad, long-term interests, even if it does not assuage the narrow, partisan frustrations of the moment. Perhaps senators should consider the longer run and broader interests when they make the rules for the coming Congress.

> *"One should realize that the U.S. Senate was undemocratic yesterday, it is undemocratic today and, unless there is a major (and altogether unlikely) radical reordering of our basic institutions, it will be undemocratic tomorrow."*

Filibuster Reform Is Not Enough to Resolve US Senate Gridlock

Sanford Levinson

Sanford Levinson is a legal scholar and professor at the University of Texas School of Law. In the following viewpoint, he contends that the November 2013 filibuster reform, which ends the use of the filibuster for presidential nominations to judicial and executive branch positions, is only a drop in the bucket when it comes to the gridlock paralyzing the US Congress. Levinson underscores the undemocratic nature of the Senate, arguing that the US Constitution gives disproportionate representation to less populated states and usurps power from the more populated ones. This allows for a tyranny of the minority. Furthermore, he maintains that filibuster reform will not prevent Republicans from filibustering US Supreme Court nominees or blocking legislation that addresses the major problems that face the nation.

As you read, consider the following questions:

1. According to Levinson, how many long-standing vacant slots on the United States Court of Appeals for the District of Columbia Circuit was President Barack Obama able to fill within a month after filibuster reforms dictated an up-or-down vote on qualified nominees?

2. With what percentage of the population represented does Levinson claim that one can reach fifty-one votes in the Senate?

3. What percentage of Americans supported enhanced background checks on firearm sales after the 2012 Sandy Hook school shooting?

On Nov. 21, 2013, the United States Senate voted to scrap the filibuster with regard to presidential nominations of executive branch officials and what the Constitution calls the judges of "inferior" courts (those below the Supreme Court). This welcome decision has already made a difference. Within a month, President Barack Obama was able to fill, with extremely competent and politically liberal judges, three years-long vacancies on the [United States Court of Appeals for the District of Columbia Circuit], often described as the second-most-important court in the country because of its special role in reviewing executive branch actions. The *New York Times* was not alone in declaring that the limitation of the filibuster represents a "return to democracy" in the United States Senate. There are two things wrong with this analysis. The mistake is to believe either that the Senate was ever democratic or that the recent decision does much to resolve the problem of gridlock in the Senate.

Historical Roots of Disproportionate Representation

As to the first, one must never forget that one of the two great compromises during the Constitutional Convention of 1787 was equal voting power of the states in the Senate (unlike in the House, where representation is proportionate to the state's population). The other so-called great compromise gave additional representation to slave states by counting slaves—even if at only three-fifths of a person each—when computing how many representatives each state would get in the House (and therefore how many votes in the Electoral College as well). James Madison was appalled by the first of these compromises, referring to equal voting power in the Senate as a "lesser evil," the greater evil being the torpedoing of the constitutional project because of the unwillingness of the small states to ratify any constitution that did not include this compromise. But an evil is still an evil, and the disproportions have only grown over the years. In 1790, Virginia had approximately 17 times the population of Delaware, then the least populous state. Today California has well over 65 times the population of Wyoming.

Indeed, in the modern United States, a majority of the roughly 313 million U.S. residents, as counted by the Census Bureau, live in a grand total of only 10 of the states, ranging from California, with its roughly 38 million people making up a bit under 1 in 8 of the national population, to North Carolina, which is edging closer to a population of 10 million. By definition, this means that a majority of the population receives only 20 percent of the votes in the Senate while the remaining 49 percent enjoys 80 percent of the votes in that body. Indeed, one can reach a majority of the Senate (51 votes) with less than 25 percent of the population represented.

There are obvious problems with the filibuster, especially as it has been recently used by Republicans in an across-the-board attempt to hobble the Obama administration. The most dramatic example is surely the relentless attempt by the Republican minority during Obama's first term to block any and all of its programs (in contrast, say, to the willingness of the late Sen. Ted Kennedy and other Democrats to work with George W. Bush on some of his key programs like No Child Left Behind or the prescription drug bill). One reason for the patent inadequacies of "Obamacare" [referring to the Patient Protection and Affordable Care Act] is the unwillingness of Senate Republicans to cooperate at all in the legislative process; it was ultimately passed by the use of an extraordinary reconciliation procedure that negated the filibuster but also made it impossible to tinker with the House legislation in beneficial ways.

Still, it is a mistake to believe that filibusters are always undemocratic even if, again by definition, those engaging in the filibuster are a minority of the voting senators. Imagine, for example, that large-state senators are taking the lead. Given that only 20 such senators could bring us beyond the majority of the electorate, a nonrandom collection of 41 filibustering senators could represent more than seventy-five percent of all Americans. To be sure, this is wildly unrealistic. It may be a long time before the senators from Texas are political allies with those from California. But one need not imagine such unlikely coalitions in order to find particular filibusters that in fact could easily claim to be representing a majority of the electorate. Benjamin Eidelson, a student at the Yale Law School, has examined hundreds of recent filibusters (or threats to filibuster) and determined that, on the basis of numbers of voters represented, Democratic-led filibusters during the Bush administration were marginally more likely to be majoritarian than Republican-led filibusters were.

An Undemocratic Institution

In any event, the Senate continues to be what it has been from day one of the United States: a dreadfully undemocratic insti-

President Barack Obama's Statement on November 2013 Filibuster Reform

All too often, we've seen a single senator or a handful of senators choose to abuse arcane procedural tactics to unilaterally block bipartisan compromises, or to prevent well-qualified, patriotic Americans from filling critical positions of public service in our system of government.

Now, at a time when millions of Americans have desperately searched for work, repeated abuse of these tactics have blocked legislation that might create jobs. They've defeated actions that would help women fighting for equal pay. They've prevented more progress than we would have liked for striving young immigrants trying to earn their citizenship. Or it's blocked efforts to end tax breaks for companies that are shipping jobs overseas. They've even been used to block commonsense and widely supported steps to protect more Americans from gun violence, even as families of victims sat in the Senate chamber and watched. And they've prevented far too many talented Americans from serving their country at a time when their country needs their talents the most.

It's harm to our economy, and it's been harmful to our democracy. And it's brought us to the point where a simple majority vote no longer seems to be sufficient for anything, even routing business through what is supposed to be the world's greatest deliberative body.

Barack Obama,
Statement on Filibuster Reform,
Whitehouse.gov, November 21, 2013.

tution that reinforces what is often a tyranny of the minority—or a tyranny of the status quo—and allows it to run roughshod over what may be the altogether defensible wishes of the majority. One should realize that the U.S. Senate was undemocratic yesterday, it is undemocratic today and, unless there is a major (and altogether unlikely) radical reordering of our basic institutions, it will be undemocratic tomorrow.

But we cannot even say that the decision of Nov. 21 has given power to the majority of the Senate, save for confirming certain appointments, however important that may be. Willful minorities retain (and will undoubtedly use) the power to prevent even the consideration, let alone the passage, of some legislation. After the Sandy Hook school shooting [a 2012 mass school shooting in Connecticut that resulted in the deaths of 26 children and adults], 90 percent public support for an enhanced ability of the government to check the backgrounds of those purchasing firearms was not enough to defeat a filibuster in the spring of 2013, and it will certainly prove ever more unavailing as memories of Sandy Hook fade. On Jan. 7, the Senate consented to a vote on a Democratic proposal that would extend unemployment benefits, but it was only the first of several required votes, and it is not clear that the bill will continue to have the 60 votes necessary to bring it to the floor for a vote. Nor can one be confident that Republicans will allow Obama proposals on energy policy or the environment—much less any bill that would require raising taxes—to come to a vote.

A Continuing Problem

And, should Justices Stephen Breyer and Ruth Bader Ginsburg offer their welcome retirements from the Supreme Court in what is, respectively, their 20th and 21st years of service, one can be absolutely confident that the Republicans in the Senate will exercise to the full their retained power to filibuster Supreme Court appointments (unless, of course, the Democrats change their minds and decide to apply majority rule with regard to those nominations). I am delighted to have Obama's three nominees to the Court of Appeals for the District of

Columbia [Circuit] join that bench, but I would be even more delighted if I believed that the Senate would be able to function effectively, passing legislation that responds to the significant problems that face us as a country. Without denigrating the importance of the judiciary or the judges who serve there, we should recognize that the problems that most Americans care (and are angry) about are not amenable to judicial resolution and require disciplined action by Congress, ideally working with the president.

The Nov. 21 decision does nothing to make one optimistic, save to demonstrate that angry Senate majorities can become sufficiently frustrated by the hyper-partisanship of their minority opponents that they will act accordingly. This suggests that the Republican Party in the Senate should in general become more willing to back off from bitter-end opposition to any of Obama's programs, lest the Democrats, having at last displayed some backbone, strike again. We shall see, but I am not holding my breath.

> *"Weakening the filibuster was a perfectly sensible goal for liberals back in the 1970s, when Democrats arguably had natural Senate and House majorities, and their main goal was to diminish the ability of Southern Democrats to cross the liberal leadership. But it makes much less sense today."*

Filibuster Reform Holds a Long-Term Political Advantage for Republicans

Sean Trende

Sean Trende is an author, journalist, and senior elections analyst for RealClearPolitics. In the following viewpoint, he maintains that comprehensive filibuster reform is a bad idea for Democrats because they hold a long-term disadvantage when it comes to controlling the House of Representatives, Senate, and the presidency. Trende explains that disadvantage comes from demographic and electoral trends, which show that the Democratic coalition is tightly packed around urban centers, while Republi-

cans are spread out across a wide swath of rural and suburban areas. Until those trends change, the Republican Party actually has the advantage in controlling the Senate and House. He also points out that Democrats should remember that the filibuster was a very effective tool for them during the George W. Bush administration.

As you read, consider the following questions:

1. How many times has a party captured control of the House of Representatives in an election held while that party also held the presidency?

2. According to Trende, what percentage of the time would Republicans win control of the Senate?

3. According to Trende, what percentage of the time would Republicans win control of the presidency?

The latest word out of the Senate is that if Republican minority leader Mitch McConnell doesn't accede to changes in the filibuster rules over the next few days, Harry Reid will invoke the so-called "nuclear option" and change the rules with 51 votes. The most likely outcome would be outlawing the filibuster on motions to proceed, thereby forcing senators to take to the floor to filibuster bills, "Mr. Smith"-style [referring to the 1939 movie *Mr. Smith Goes to Washington*].

This move, and the overwhelming progressive enthusiasm for it, are head-scratchers. Over the short to medium term (and no one can really see beyond that), the filibuster probably helps the Democrats more than it helps the Republicans. Before going any further, let me make clear that the following argument is couched purely in terms of political advantage and ability to move the agenda. I think there's a lot to be said for what we might call the small-"c" conservative arguments for the filibuster: requiring 60 votes creates the need for some sort of consensus before legislation moves through, and the chances of a destabilizing period of time where parties trade majorities and implement wildly divergent agendas willy-nilly are greatly diminished. In that sense, the filibuster helps the entire country, and both parties should be pleased with it.

The Politics of the Filibuster

That said, let's analyze the politics of the filibuster, beginning with the following observation: The filibuster doesn't really matter unless you control the House of Representatives, Senate, and presidency—what we might call the "trifecta." Even if Reid were to lower the number of votes needed to move legislation through the Senate to 20 votes, it still wouldn't significantly advance the Democratic cause in Congress, because the Republican House acts as an effective filibuster. Similarly, when Republicans hold the presidency, a veto would stop any legislation.

Sure, a Democratic Senate sans filibuster could pass legislation that might make a Republican House or president uncomfortable, and would be able to prevent its most vulnerable members from casting difficult votes (Blanche Lincoln, for example, would not have had to cast the deciding vote for Obamacare [referring to the Patient Protection and Affordable Care Act], and Democrats might still hold her seat). And to the extent that Republicans might try to block judges or cabinet appointees, the filibuster matters. But that is a two-way street (Lincoln Chafee might still be around had he not had to vote for parts of President Bush's agenda), and in terms of advancing a progressive agenda, without the trifecta, the filibuster is largely superfluous.

So here's the problem for Democrats: Republican trifectas are more likely, all other things being equal, than Democratic trifectas, at least in the near future. Let's assume for the sake of argument that Democrats have a structural demographic edge in the presidency (I don't agree, but let's assume). Even the most rabid defenders of what we might call the Emerging

197

Democratic Majority thesis concede that Republicans will still win the presidency if there is a recession, unpopular war, or other national upheaval.

Those contingencies happen with some regularity. So setting aside the fact that in the long run, presidential races sort out much the same way as do coin flips (the parties have each won the popular vote 20 times since the Republican Party was founded), let's assume that in the short to medium term Democrats will win the presidency two-thirds of the time.

The Case of the US House of Representatives

The House is another matter entirely. While it isn't impossible for Democrats to retake the House (even in 2014), it is difficult. This is a subject worthy of a separate article, but given the current redistricting lines, and given how the Democrats' coalition has sorted out into tightly packed geographic constituencies (urban liberals, minorities crammed into minority-majority districts), it makes a switch unlikely except in wave years.

Take 2012 as an example. With an electorate that featured one of the most favorable demographic tilts toward Democrats in recent memory, with a president winning by a decent margin, and with Democrats even winning the popular vote for the House by a point, Republicans won the third largest number of seats they have enjoyed after an election since the 1920s.

The fact that we assume Democrats will dominate presidential elections works against them here as well. Since we began regularly holding our House elections in even years (around the Civil War), a party has *captured* control of the House in an election held while that party also held the presidency exactly once: 1948.

So let's assign Democrats a 20 percent chance of winning the House. That leaves us with the Senate. The Senate is a *natural* GOP gerrymander. Consider: Mitt Romney lost by 3.8 points, but still carried 24 states. John McCain lost by 7.3 points, but carried 22 states. On the other hand, when John Kerry lost by only 2.5 points, he carried just 19 states. Twenty-seven states currently have Republican PVIs [partisan voting index], meaning that in a completely neutral environment, we'd expect them to vote for a Republican.

An Advantage for Republicans

Over the long term, this translates into an advantage for Republicans, since presidential results are fairly predictive of where Senate races shake out. Obviously there are shortcomings with this approach: Democrats run better in West Virginia than recent presidential results would suggest, while Republicans run better in Maine. Poor candidate choice (think Alexi Giannoulias in Illinois, Todd Akin in Missouri) can disproportionately hurt the parties, while unfavorable environments combined with overexposure (à la Republicans in 2008, Democrats in 1980) can result in disaster. But over time, these contingencies should cancel each other out, and Republicans should tend to win control.

To try to quantify this a little bit better, let's do something a little bit outside the box and run a rudimentary Monte Carlo simulation for Senate races. This is an old statistical technique (popularized recently by Nate Silver at *FiveThirtyEight*), which more or less allows a researcher to generate hypothetical results from a set of variables.

So we might say that a Democrat in Colorado can be expected to win 53 percent of the vote on average, and will be within five points of that 95 percent of the time, while a Republican in Idaho will be within five points of 63 percent of the vote 19 times out of 20. Monte Carlo simulations will generate random results within those confines.

If you run 100 simulations, the Democrat should, on average, get 53 percent of the vote in Colorado, and will almost always be between 48 percent and 58 percent, while the Republican will almost always be between 58 percent and 68 percent in Idaho. If you run 1,000 simulations, you would be able to get a pretty good estimate of how often Republicans would win both seats in that hypothetical two-seat Senate (about 27 percent of the time).

The trick here is estimating what percentage of the vote a state will tend to cast for a Republican, all other things being equal. Presidential performance gives a decent base line. The rest—retirements and incumbency, political environment, exposure, candidate quality—matter in the short term, but should cancel out over time.

Of course, President Obama's numbers likely overstate Democratic strength somewhat in Illinois, and understate it in West Virginia. To help correct for that, we'll take the average of the past five presidential elections in each state.

But a state that gave the Democrats, say, 62 percent of the vote on average wouldn't elect a Republican 62 percent of the time; that number would approach zero. Likewise, a state that gave Democrats 45 percent of the vote on average probably wouldn't result in a Democratic win more than one time in four. To correct for this, a simple linear transformation is applied to these averages, effectively making a state that gave Democrats 60 percent a sure-fire win for that party, while the opposite is true for states that gave Democrats less than 40 percent of the vote.

Finally, I took the standard deviation of these five elections for each state. The basic idea is that a state that gave Democrats 52 percent of the vote in all five elections shouldn't be expected to move much off of that 52 percent average, but a state like West Virginia, where results have ranged between 36 percent and 58 percent of the vote for Democrats, should be allowed to move substantially off the median.

The Results

Using these as our metric, and running our simulation 2,000 times, we find Republicans winning control of the Senate 74 percent of the time, with 51 seats on average. This is encouraging, since they have won control of the Senate after six of the past 10 elections, and have won 50 seats on average during those same elections.

Over the course of 2,000 elections, things would probably end up pretty close to what our simulation predicts; for that matter, if 2008 hadn't been such an unusually bad environment for Republicans (and if Ted Stevens hadn't been convicted of a felony on the eve of the election), our simulation would likely be spot-on. And even if this is a touch too optimistic for Republicans, our House and presidential estimates are probably a touch too optimistic for Democrats.

Already we can see the problem for the Democrats—control of just the Senate is very difficult for them to maintain over the long haul. At the same time, Republicans should never achieve a filibuster-proof majority; the best they do in our simulation is 59 seats, once every 1,000 elections.

Moreover, if our estimates are right (Republicans win the presidency 33 percent of the time, the Senate 74 percent of the time, and the House 80 percent of the time), Republicans should win the trifecta 20 percent of the time, versus just 3 percent of the time for Democrats. And again, Republicans held the trifecta after three of the last 10 elections, while Democrats won it in just one (held in extraordinarily favorable circumstances). In truth, the odds are probably a little better for both parties to win the trifecta, since these elections aren't completely independent variables, but that affects both parties and does little to affect the underlying observation about the relative likelihood of Republican trifectas vis-à-vis Democratic ones.

A Senseless Move

Weakening the filibuster was a perfectly sensible goal for liberals back in the 1970s, when Democrats arguably had natural Senate and House majorities, and their main goal was to diminish the ability of Southern Democrats to cross the liberal leadership. But it makes much less sense today. Yes, Democrats can point to some cherished action items that were lost in the first half of Obama's term (the public option, card check).

At the same time, however, the filibuster greatly restrained Republicans' ability to implement their agenda during the Bush years. Without it, they probably would have passed tort reform, ANWR [Arctic National Wildlife Refuge] drilling, Social Security privatization, school vouchers, made the Bush tax cuts permanent, and further diminished unions' ability to organize. Republicans might have passed immigration reform, President Bush almost certainly would have placed Miguel Estrada on the Supreme Court, and Hispanics might be a more reliably Republican voting group. In short, in terms of policy changes, the filibuster has probably inhibited Republicans more over the past decade than Democrats.

Overall, that's what makes the move such a head-scratcher. There's no immediate benefit for Democrats, little short- or medium-term benefit, and some potentially catastrophic downsides for them during that time frame. Unless their coalition changes in the coming decade or two, Democrats are probably more likely to rue these changes than to celebrate them.

| *"There's plenty of hypocrisy on both sides of the aisle here."*

Filibuster Reform Does Not Benefit Any Party in the Long Run

Gene Healy

Gene Healy is an author, political commentator, and vice president of the Cato Institute. In the following viewpoint, he finds limited filibuster reform enacted in 2013 had some merit. The reform, which ended the use of the filibuster for presidential nominations to judicial and executive branch positions in the Senate, makes it easier for the president's nominees to get confirmed. It also allows the filibuster for Supreme Court nominees, which Healy feels is important to prevent the confirmation of radical candidates. However, he worries that this limited filibuster reform will inevitably lead to more comprehensive reform, known as the "nuclear option," which would eliminate the filibuster for legislation in the Senate. Healy argues that no one will win if that happens because the Senate was designed to be delib-

erative and cautious. He argues that employing the nuclear option would lead to the passage of ill-considered and extreme laws that could damage the country.

As you read, consider the following questions:

1. According to Healy, what was the vote on the November 2013 filibuster reform in the Senate?

2. According to the viewpoint, what did constitutional scholars argue in their 2010 article, "In Praise of Supreme Court Filibusters"?

3. What did James Madison explain in "Federalist No. 62," according to the author?

Man, I'm so old, I remember when conservatives used to call what Senate majority leader Harry Reid, D-Nev., just did the "constitutional option." By a vote of 52 to 48, with only three Democrats defecting, on Thursday [in November 2013], the Senate, led by Reid, changed the rules to prevent filibusters of virtually all presidential nominees except Supreme Court justices.

By a simple majority vote—rather than the two-thirds that Senate rules require—Reid changed the rules mid-game, to prevent minority-party "obstruction" of the president's nominees. Back in spring 2005, when President George W. Bush had just won reelection, and Karl Rove-ian triumphalism was in the air, Republicans came close to banning judicial filibusters. Though irate Democrats preferred the term "nuclear option," the GOP called the majority-vote rule change "the constitutional option." (Oddly, the Senate Republican Policy Committee [RPC] report adopting that moniker seems to have vanished from the RPC's website).

This time around, the Democrats have adopted Republican messaging to gain support for the rule change, and there's nothing but wailing and gnashing of teeth from Republicans who once considered "an up-or-down vote" on presidential nominees a matter of high principle.

It Could Be Worse

There's plenty of hypocrisy on both sides of the aisle here. But as the constitutional scholars John O. McGinnis and Michael B. Rappaport argued in a 2010 article, "In Praise of Supreme Court Filibusters," to "avoid obvious partisanship," we should look at confirmation rules as if behind "a veil of ignorance" about whether the Red Team or Blue Team currently holds the levers of power.

From that perspective, where the Senate drew the line on Thursday—eliminating the judicial filibuster for executive branch posts and lower federal courts, but preserving it for the Supreme Court—is nothing to celebrate, but it could be a lot worse.

Given life tenure and the court's de facto ability to "legislate from the bench," it's important to preserve the option to filibuster Supreme Court nominees. But as McGinnis and Rappaport point out, "inferior federal courts by themselves ordinarily cannot entrench new constitutional norms against the democratic process," thus here the problem presented by unelected judges' power to reshape the law "is far less acute."

When it comes to executive branch nominees, the argument that the president, with advice and consent of the Senate, gets to pick the people who work for him, has some merit. More "up-or-down votes" here might check abuse of recess appointments and help encourage the Supreme Court to restore limits on presidential power to do an end run around Senate confirmation.

But there's a real danger that the Senate's nuclear brinksmanship ends up eliminating the legislative filibuster as well. As James Madison explained in "Federalist [No.] 62," the Senate itself was designed in part to curb "the facility and excess of lawmaking."

Playing with Nukes

As I warned back in 2005, a nuclear "second strike from a future Democratic majority could be used to prevent minorities from filibustering legislation that the majority favors."

That option is on the table, apparently. "For a lot of us," says freshman senator Chris Murphy, D-Conn., "this is only halfway to the finish line: We should get rid of the filibuster for legislation as well as nominations."

In fact, Senate Republican leader Mitch McConnell of Kentucky has (regretfully, to be sure) threatened to do just that should the GOP recapture the Senate. "Let them do it," Reid remarked. "Why in the world would we care?"

Serious political movements shouldn't try to knock down all the barriers to power whenever they temporarily enjoy it, because nothing is permanent in politics save the drive for more federal power, and the weapons you forge may someday be detonated by the other side.

Play with nukes, and sometimes you get burned.

Periodical and Internet Sources Bibliography

The following articles have been selected to supplement the diverse views presented in this chapter.

Aaron Belkin	"The Way to a More Responsive Congress," *New York Times*, November 22, 2013.
Tyler Creighton	"Filibuster Reform: Given the Gridlock, It Had to Happen," *Boston Globe*, December 23, 2013.
Tom Daschle and Trent Lott	"Filibuster Reform and Other Fixes for the Senate," *Wall Street Journal*, June 24, 2014.
Joshua Green	"McConnell Says Reid's Filibuster Reforms Will Destroy the Senate. Not Really," *Bloomberg Businessweek*, July 15, 2013.
KC Johnson	"Filibuster Reform Is Needed, but Won't End Partisan Gridlock," *U.S. News & World Report*, November 27, 2012.
Suzy Khimm	"Would Reforming the Filibuster Really End Gridlock?," *Washington Post*, July 20, 2012.
Thomas E. Mann	"The Senate After Filibuster Reform," Reuters, November 25, 2013.
Napp Nazworth	"Was Harry Reid Just Bluffing on Filibuster Reform?," *Christian Post*, January 25, 2013.
John Nichols	"Senate Deal Breaks Some Gridlock, but This Isn't the Filibuster Reform That's Needed," *Nation*, July 16, 2013.
Jeremy W. Peters	"New Senate Rules to Curtail the Excesses of a Filibuster," *New York Times*, January 24, 2013.
Samantha Paige Rosen	"Wendy Davis's Filibuster: Keeping Gridlock Alive," *Huffington Post*, June 27, 2013.

For Further Discussion

Chapter 1

1. Russell E. Saltzman contends that gridlock is actually good for government. What does the author cite as the major benefits of gridlock? Do you agree with his argument? Explain.

2. Michael A. Cohen claims that the American political system is dysfunctional. Based on Cohen's arguments, do you agree or disagree? Explain.

Chapter 2

1. Emily Badger suggests that divided government is a major cause of gridlock. Do you agree or disagree with the author, and why? Do you think more moderate members of Congress from each party would help resolve government gridlock? Explain.

2. Mark Kesselman believes that the gridlock in Washington is caused by the Tea Party. In your view, does Kesselman provide sufficient evidence to support his claim? Why, or why not?

3. Michael Kranish reports on the role partisan media plays in political polarization. What are the author's main arguments in the viewpoint? Do you agree or disagree with Kranish? Explain.

Chapter 3

1. According to John B. Anderson, election reforms would allow voters to have better representation in Congress. In your opinion, does Anderson present a compelling argument? Explain your answer. Do you think a third US political party would alleviate or exacerbate gridlock? Explain.

2. Both Ned Barnett and Richard A. Epstein address the possibility of changing the Constitution. What is each author's stance on the subject? With which author do you agree, and why?

3. Susan Page cites three measures that could help repair the government. What are these measures? Do you believe they would have a positive impact on the government? Explain your reasoning.

Chapter 4

1. Harry Reid makes his case for filibuster reform. Why does Reid believe such reform is necessary? Do you agree or disagree with his argument, and why?

2. According to Gene Healy, filibuster reform benefits neither Democrats nor Republicans. Based on Healy's argument, do you think if Republicans gained a majority in the Senate in the future they would support further filibuster reform? Explain your reasoning.

Organizations to Contact

The editors have compiled the following list of organizations concerned with the issues debated in this book. The descriptions are derived from materials provided by the organizations. All have publications or information available for interested readers. The list was compiled on the date of publication of the present volume; the information provided here may change. Be aware that many organizations take several weeks or longer to respond to inquiries, so allow as much time as possible.

American Enterprise Institute (AEI)
1150 Seventeenth Street NW, Washington, DC 20036
(202) 862-5800 • fax: (202) 862-7177
website: www.aei.org

The American Enterprise Institute (AEI) is a private, non-profit, nonpartisan community of scholars dedicated to expanding liberty, increasing individual opportunity, and strengthening free enterprise. The institute publishes numerous newsletters and the online magazine the *American*, which is available on the AEI website. Also on its website, AEI offers testimony, commentary, speeches, and articles, including "Can We—and Do We Want to—Avoid Gridlock?"

Bipartisan Policy Center
1225 Eye Street NW, Suite 1000, Washington, DC 20005
(202) 204-2400 • fax: (202) 637-9220
e-mail: bipartisaninfo@bipartisanpolicy.org
website: bipartisanpolicy.org

The Bipartisan Policy Center is a nonprofit organization that promotes bipartisanship, addresses the nation's key challenges, and drives policy solutions. It launched the Commission on Political Reform to examine America's partisan political divide and to advocate for reforms that would improve the political process and eliminate polarized politics. The organization's website includes an In the News section with links to articles such as "To End Partisan Gridlock," "Fixing Washington's Political Gridlock," and "Gridlock Has Cost U.S. Billions, and the Meter Is Still Running."

Brennan Center for Justice

161 Avenue of the Americas, 12th Floor, New York, NY 10013
(646) 292-8310 • fax: (212) 463-7308
e-mail: brennancenter@nyu.edu
website: www.brennancenter.org

The Brennan Center for Justice at New York University School of Law is a nonpartisan law and policy institute working to improve democracy and justice. Named after Supreme Court justice William J. Brennan Jr., the institute focuses on a number of issues, including government and court reform. Among its publications are "Filibuster Abuse" and "Curbing Filibuster Abuse." The center recently held a conference to address the problems of government dysfunction and polarization. A report titled "The Governing Crisis: Exploring Options," which summarizes seven panel discussions held during the conference, can be downloaded from the center's website.

Brookings Institution

1775 Massachusetts Avenue NW, Washington, DC 20036
(202) 797-6000
e-mail: communications@brookings.edu
website: www.brookings.edu

The Brookings Institution is a nonprofit organization devoted to independent research and innovative policy solutions. Its mission is to conduct high-quality, independent research and to then provide innovative, practical recommendations that can strengthen American democracy. Its website contains information on US politics and offers a variety of publications, such as the articles "Polarized We Govern?" and "How We're Doing Amid Policy Gridlock."

Cato Institute

1000 Massachusetts Avenue NW, Washington, DC 20001
(202) 842-0200
website: www.cato.org

The Cato Institute is a public policy think tank dedicated to the principles of individual liberty, limited government, free markets, and peace. Cato analyzes a wide range of issues, including government gridlock. Articles, such as "The Constitution, Gridlock and American Politics" and "Please—Enough with the Gridlock Lament," as well as reports and policy studies, can be found on the Cato website. In addition, Cato publishes periodicals such as the *Cato Journal*, the *Cato Policy Report*, and the quarterly *Regulation* magazine.

Common Cause

1133 Nineteenth Street NW, 9th Floor
Washington, DC 20036
(202) 833-1200
website: www.commoncause.org

Founded in 1970, Common Cause is a nonpartisan, nonprofit advocacy organization that encourages citizen participation in democracy and promotes an honest, open, and accountable government. It has nearly four hundred thousand members and supporters, with offices in thirty-five states. The organization's website contains information related to government gridlock, including the report "The New Nullification at Work: Executive Branch Nominations and the Tactics of Obstruction."

Heritage Foundation

214 Massachusetts Avenue NE, Washington, DC 20002-4999
(202) 546-4400
e-mail: info@heritage.org
website: www.heritage.org

Founded in 1973, the Heritage Foundation is a conservative public policy research institute that supports the principles of free enterprise, limited government, individual freedom, and traditional American values. Its website features *The Daily Signal,* a news platform that provides policy and political news as well as commentary and political analysis. Also available on its website are position papers, fact sheets, reports, and articles, including "Filibuster 'Reform' Is a Partisan Power Grab."

Hoover Institution

434 Galvez Mall, Stanford University
Stanford, CA 94305-6010
(650) 723-1754
website: www.hoover.org

The Hoover Institution is a public policy research center focused on the study of economics, politics, history, political economy, and international affairs. Located at Stanford University, the institution features renowned scholars and a library and archives. Its website offers a variety of publications, including *Hoover Daily Report, Hoover Digest,* and *Defining Ideas.*

No Labels

PO Box 25429, Washington, DC 20027
(202) 588-1990
website: www.nolabels.org

No Labels is a citizens' movement of Democrats, Republicans, and Independents who promote a new politics of problem solving. The organization strives to bring together political leaders and political parties to create solutions to the nation's problems. On its website, the Make Congress Work section features a twelve-point plan for breaking gridlock, promoting constructive discussion, and reducing polarization in Congress. Additionally, its website features a blog with links to articles such as "Four Smart Ways to Reduce US Political Gridlock, Our Biggest Economic Problem."

Office of Congressional Ethics (OCE)

US House of Representatives, 425 Third Street SW, Suite 1110
Washington, DC 20024

(202) 225-9739 • fax: (202) 226-0997
e-mail: oce@mail.house.gov
website: oce.house.gov

Formed in 2008 by the US House of Representatives as an independent investigative agency, the Office of Congressional Ethics (OCE) is charged with reviewing allegations of misconduct against members, officers, and staff of the United States House of Representatives and reporting such allegations to the House Committee on Ethics. The OCE, made up of a nonpartisan panel of private citizens, seeks to help the House uphold high standards of conduct. Its website provides a variety of information, including a citizens' guide, quarterly reports, press advisories, and a blog.

Pew Research Center
1615 L Street NW, Suite 700, Washington, DC   20036
(202) 419-4300 • fax: (202) 419-4349
website: www.pewresearch.org

The Pew Research Center is a nonpartisan "fact tank" that provides information on the issues, attitudes, and trends shaping America and the world. It conducts public opinion polls and social science research, reports and analyzes news, and holds forums and briefings, but it does not take positions on policy issues. The US Politics section on its website provides information, survey reports, and articles on a wide range of topics, including government gridlock and political polarization. Its reports include "Political Polarization in the American Public."

Project on Government Oversight (POGO)
1100 G Street NW, Suite 500, Washington, DC   20005
(202) 347-1122 • fax: (202) 347-1116
e-mail: info@pogo.org
website: www.pogo.org

Founded in 1981, the Project on Government Oversight (POGO) is a nonpartisan, independent watchdog that supports government reforms. POGO's mission is to investigate corruption, misconduct, and conflicts of interest to achieve a more effective, accountable federal government. The group's website contains a publications library that provides access to reports, testimony, databases, and more. In addition, its website offers *The (POGO) Blog* with articles such as "5 Steps to Curing Election Dysfunction."

Bibliography of Books

Kevin Arceneaux and Martin Johnson — *Changing Minds or Changing Channels?: Partisan News in an Age of Choice.* Chicago, IL: University of Chicago Press, 2013.

Richard A. Arenberg and Robert B. Dove — *Defending the Filibuster: The Soul of the Senate.* Bloomington, IN: Indiana University Press, 2012.

H. Woody Brock — *American Gridlock: Why the Right and Left Are Both Wrong: Commonsense 101 Solutions to the Economic Crises.* Hoboken, NJ: John Wiley & Sons, 2012.

Michael Charney — *Tea with the Mad Hatter: Musings on Politics, the Tea Party, and America's Rampant Electile Dysfunction.* Bedford, NH: Riddle Brook Publishing, 2012.

Michael S. Cummings, ed. — *American Political Thought.* 7th ed. Los Angeles, CA: CQ Press, 2014.

Lawrence Dorfman — *The Snark Handbook: Politics & Government Edition: Gridlock, Red Tape, and Other Insults to We the People.* New York: Skyhorse Publishing, 2012.

Payne Edwards — *Gridlock: Why We're in It and How to Get Out.* Kissimmee, FL: Signalman Publishing, 2012.

Patrick J. Egan — *Partisan Priorities: How Issue Ownership Drives and Distorts American Politics.* New York: Cambridge University Press, 2013.

Richard J. Ellis and Michael Nelson, eds. — *Debating Reform: Conflicting Perspectives on How to Fix the American Political System.* Los Angeles, CA: CQ Press, 2013.

Marcus E. Ethridge — *The Case for Gridlock: Democracy, Organized Power, and the Legal Foundations of American Government.* Lanham, MD: Lexington Books, 2011.

Kirby Goidel — *America's Failing Experiment: How We the People Have Become the Problem.* Lanham, MD: Rowman & Littlefield, 2013.

Philip K. Howard — *The Rule of Nobody: Saving America from Dead Laws and Broken Government.* New York: W.W. Norton & Company, 2014.

Jon Huntsman, ed. — *No Labels: A Shared Vision for a Stronger America.* New York: Diversion Books, 2014.

Carl J. Jarvis — *The United States of Dysfunction: America's Political Crisis and What Ordinary Citizens Can Do About It.* Houston, TX: BKSC Media Group, 2014.

Matthew Levendusky	*How Partisan Media Polarize America.* Chicago, IL: University of Chicago Press, 2013.
Thomas E. Mann and Norman J. Ornstein	*It's Even Worse than It Looks: How the American Constitutional System Collided with the New Politics of Extremism.* New York: Basic Books, 2012.
David R. Mayhew	*Partisan Balance: Why Political Parties Don't Kill the U.S. Constitutional System.* Princeton, NJ: Princeton University Press, 2011.
Mark Meckler and Jenny Beth Martin	*Tea Party Patriots: The Second American Revolution.* New York: Henry Holt and Company, 2012.
Rand Paul	*The Tea Party Goes to Washington.* New York: Center Street, 2011.
Dustin D. Romney	*Rule of Law: Why and How We Must Amend the Constitution.* Seattle, WA: CreateSpace, 2014.
Manabu Saeki	*The Other Side of Gridlock: Policy Stability and Supermajoritarianism in U.S. Lawmaking.* Albany: State University of New York Press, 2011.
Scot Schraufnagel	*Third Party Blues: The Truth and Consequences of Two-Party Dominance.* New York: Routledge, 2011.
Peter H. Schuck	*Why Government Fails So Often: And How It Can Do Better.* Princeton, NJ: Princeton University Press, 2014.

Hedrick Smith — *Who Stole the American Dream?* New York: Random House, 2013.

Olympia Snowe — *Fighting for Common Ground: How We Can Fix the Stalemate in Congress.* New York: Weinstein Books, 2013.

James I. Wallner — *The Death of Deliberation: Partisanship and Polarization in the United States Senate.* Lanham, MD: Rowman & Littlefield, 2013.

Ned Witting — *Political Gridlock: It's Time for a Reboot!* Bloomington, IN: AuthorHouse, 2014.

Bob Woodward — *The Price of Politics.* New York: Simon & Schuster, 2013.

Index

G